STUDENT UNIT GUIDE

NEW EDITION

AQA(B) A2 Psychology Unit 3

Child Development and Applied Options

Julie McLoughlin

PHILIP ALLAN

Philip Allan Updates, an imprint of Hodder Education, an Hachette UK company, Market Place, Deddington, Oxfordshire OX15 OSE

Orders
Bookpoint Ltd, 130 Milton Park, Abingdon, Oxfordshire OX14 4SB
tel: 01235 827827
fax: 01235 400401
e-mail: education@bookpoint.co.uk
Lines are open 9.00 a.m.–5.00 p.m., Monday to Saturday, with a 24-hour message answering service. You can also order through the Philip Allan Updates website: www.philipallan.co.uk

© Julie McLoughlin 2012

ISBN 978-1-4441-6227-1

First printed 2012
Impression number 5 4 3
Year 2016 2015

Cover photo: Andreas Karellas/Fotolia

Typeset by Integra, India

Printed in India

Hachette UK's policy is to use papers that are natural, renewable and recyclable products and made from wood grown in sustainable forests. The logging and manufacturing processes are expected to conform to the environmental regulations of the country of origin.

P2033

Contents

Content Guidance

Questions & Answers

Getting the most from this book

Questions & Answers

Exam-style questions

Examiner comments on the questions
Tips on what you need to do to gain full marks, indicated by the icon ⓔ.

Sample student answers
Practise the questions, then look at the student answers that follow each set of questions.

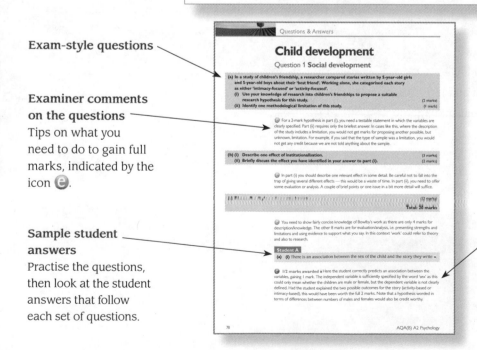

Examiner commentary on sample student answers
Find out how many marks each answer would be awarded in the exam and then read the examiner comments (preceded by the icon ⓔ) following each student answer

Annotations that link back to points made in the student answers show exactly how and where marks are gained or lost.

About this book

This is a guide to Unit 3 of the AQA(B) A2 psychology specification. The guide is intended as a revision aid rather than as a textbook. The purpose of the guide is to summarise the content, to explain how the content will be assessed, to look at the types of questions to expect, and to consider specimen answers.

There are eight topic areas in Unit 3 and you have to answer questions on three of these topics in your examination. You must choose one topic from the child development section and two from the applied options section. The choice of topics is shown in Table 1.

Table 1 Choice of topics

Child development (choose one topic)	Applied options (choose two topics)
Social development	Cognition and law
Cognitive development	Schizophrenia and mood disorders
Moral development	Stress and stress management
	Substance abuse
	Forensic psychology

For each of these topics, this guide will cover the following:
- the specification content, which tells you exactly what you need to know and learn
- appropriate content relevant to the topic. This gives you minimal coverage of the topic, as you should already have covered the details in your studies. The focus is on key terms and concepts, key theories and studies and evaluation points. The content here is not the only appropriate material; textbooks will cover the topics in various ways and probably give much more detail as well as alternative studies.
- a sample question in the style of AQA(B) A2 questions, similar to those that you might expect to see on real examination papers
- an analysis of how the question should be tackled and what the examiners are looking for in an answer
- a typical grade-D student answer (student A), together with examiner comments showing where the marks have been gained and lost, drawing attention to any errors and giving suggestions as to how the answers might be improved or elaborated to get extra marks
- a typical grade-A student answer (student B), followed by examiner comments that show which points are especially creditworthy.

If you read these sample answers and comments carefully, you will learn a lot about what you need to do to present a really effective answer in the examination.

How to use this guide

First, check your class notes and revision notes against the content presented here to make sure that you have all the right material for your revision. Then look at a sample question to see how the examination is structured and what is required. Try to answer the question, and then examine the sample answers and comments to see where credit can be gained and lost. The sample answers are not intended as model answers but as tools to help you understand what makes a good answer. Finally, you should review your own answer in the light of what you have read and consider how your own response to the question might be improved.

Content Guidance

In this section, content guidance is offered on the topic areas of child development and applied options. Each topic begins with a summary of the AQA Specification B requirements for Unit 3. This is followed by a brief account of the theories and studies that make up the unit content.

Knowledge of appropriate theories and studies is essential for the A2 examination. It is also important to be able to assess their value, and this is done here with regular 'Evaluation' features that provide criticisms of both.

Names and publication dates have been given when referring to research studies. The full details for these studies are normally available in textbooks, should you wish to research the topic further.

Child development

Social development

Early relationships

Summary specification content

Attachment and the role of caregiver–infant interactions in the development of attachment, including reference to human and animal studies. Function of attachment. Secure and insecure attachments. Measuring attachment.

Possible short-term and long-term consequences of privation and deprivation.

Romanian orphan studies: effects of institutionalisation, age-related benefits of adoption (Rutter et al.).

The work of Bowlby, Schaffer, Ainsworth and van Ijzendoorn.

The role of caregiver–infant interactions

Various aspects of caregiver–infant interactions help to develop and maintain attachment. These include imitation, interactional synchrony, physical contact, modified language and sensitive responsiveness.

Imitation

Melzoff and Moore (1977) found that 2- to 3-week-old babies would imitate adults' facial expressions and movements. They concluded that even tiny babies will spontaneously imitate face and hand movements.

> **Examiner tip**
> In questions on infant–caregiver interaction you should focus on the role that these interactions might play in the development of attachment. You must do more than simply describe the behaviours.

Interactional synchrony

Condon and Sander (1974) analysed babies' movements when an adult was speaking to them. They found that babies would move in time with the conversation and 'take turns' — reciprocal behaviour. Isabella et al. (1989) found more interactional synchrony in securely attached mother–baby pairs.

Physical contact

Klaus and Kennell (1976) suggested that immediate contact and skin-to-skin stimulation in the period after birth was important for the formation of a bond.

Modified language (motherese)

Motherese is a slow, high-pitched, repetitive way of speaking to young babies that involves short, simple sentences and varying tone. It aids communication and may contribute to effective turn-taking, aiding attachment.

Sensitive responsiveness

Ainsworth (1978) found that the type and quality of attachment depended on the behaviour of the mother (see Ainsworth's strange situation on p. 9).

Evaluation

- Imitation may not be intentional communication.
- Cross-cultural work suggests interactional synchrony is not linked to attachment (LeVine et al., 1994).
- Immediate physical contact is not essential for attachment.
- Adults use motherese with all babies and young children. There is no direct evidence that it affects attachment.
- Cross-cultural evidence suggests that sensitive responsiveness is not always necessary for secure attachment.

Animal research

Studies with monkeys suggest that infant–caregiver interaction is important for the development of attachment.

Study: Harlow (1959)

Harlow studied infant rhesus monkeys separated from their mothers at birth. The caged infants had two substitute mothers: a soft cloth mother and a wire mother with a feeding bottle. The infants spent more time with the cloth mother, visiting the wire mother just for food. When later introduced to normal monkeys, the separated infants showed delinquent behaviour; they were aggressive and unable to form relationships. Harlow concluded that attachment depends on physical comfort more than on food and that a lack of attachment leads to antisocial behaviour.

reciprocal behaviour behaviour that either elicits a response from another person or which is produced in response to the behaviour of another person

Knowledge check 1
Name five types of caregiver interactions that might play a role in the development of attachment.

Evaluation

- Harlow's research caused distress to the infant monkeys.
- It may be inappropriate to generalise from monkeys to human attachment.

Function of attachment

- Cupboard-love theory — babies attach to those who feed them. Harlow's study suggests this is incorrect.
- Survival theory — according to evolutionary theory, attachment aids survival. Observations show how young animals often attach instinctively to the first large moving object they see (imprinting) (Lorenz, 1935). Psychoanalytic theorists (e.g. Bowlby, 1969) proposed that human infants have an innate, instinctual drive to keep proximity to the caregiver.
- Communication theory — Bower (1979) suggested that infants choose to attach to the person with whom they can best communicate; the person who is most sensitive to the child's communication. This explanation links to Ainsworth's views about sensitive responsiveness.
- The internal working model — Bowlby (1969) proposed that a child's earliest attachment provides an internal working model of relationships, which is used as a framework for future relationships. Dunn (1993) argued that the concept is too general to be useful.

Measuring attachment: secure and insecure attachments

We shall consider three methods: the strange situation (observational method), the adult attachment interview (interview method) and the attachment Q-sort (psychological test).

The strange situation (Ainsworth)

Ainsworth et al. (1978) carried out a controlled observation of brief separations from the mother. In a series of 3-minute episodes, infant and mother were observed with the researcher, the researcher left the room, a stranger entered, the mother left, the mother returned etc. Behaviours such as proximity seeking and maintenance of proximity were recorded. Infants were classified as securely attached (65%), anxious avoidant or anxious resistant (15–20% each). Ainsworth concluded that there are different types of attachments and the type depends on the mother's sensitivity and responsiveness.

Evaluation

- Category percentages are similar in many cultures.
- Proximity seeking may not be a valid measure. Secure infants do not always stay close to the mother and are happy to explore (Cassidy, 1986).
- Ainsworth neglected temperament, family background etc.
- Fraley and Spieker (2003) suggested two dimensions to attachment: proximity seeking versus avoidance, and anger/resistance versus emotional confidence.

Examiner tip

Remember the two very important findings from the Harlow study: (i) Infants attach for comfort rather than for food; (ii) maternal privation leads to serious long-term consequences such as delinquency. Sometimes you might need to focus more on one conclusion than the other.

Knowledge check 2

Why is it important for a young infant to develop a good internal working model?

The strange situation (van Ijzendoorn)

Van Ijzendoorn and Kroonenberg (1988) compared 32 strange situation studies from eight countries. They found more anxious-avoidant attachments in Germany and more anxious-resistant attachments in Israel and Japan. This suggests different child-rearing practices affect the type of attachment. De Wolff and van Ijzendoorn (1997) found only a weak link between the mother's sensitivity and security of attachment.

The adult attachment interview (Main et al., 1985)

The adult attachment interview is a 1-hour interview with 15 open questions about attachment experience. Responses are categorised as insecure-dismissing, autonomous-secure, insecure-preoccupied or unresolved. Autonomous-secure individuals have securely attached children.

The attachment Q-sort

This involves sorting a set of 90 cards into piles according to how true the card description is of the child's behaviour. An attachment score is then calculated.

Consequences of privation and deprivation

Privation is never having had a secure relationship with an attachment figure. Animal research (e.g. Harlow's monkey study on p. 8) showed that privated monkeys became delinquent and aggressive. Case studies of severely neglected individuals provide evidence for the effects of privation on humans. Genie (Curtiss, 1977) was neglected until the age of 13 years. She was physically underdeveloped and had no language skills. Although her condition improved when taken into care, she never really recovered from her years of privation.

Study: Koluchova (1991)

Koluchova studied twin boys who had been locked in a cellar from the age of 18 months. At 7 years they went into care and were later fostered. By 10 years their IQ level was average. They had normal family attachments. As adults, they had jobs and families. The years of privation seem to have been overcome.

Deprivation is having a secure relationship with an attachment figure and then losing it. Short-term consequences include a sequence of behaviour known as protest–despair–detachment.

This was shown by Robertson and Robertson (1968), who filmed young children going into care. Schaffer (1996) suggested that boys suffer most in separations. Other factors are a difficult temperament, previous family conflict and repeat separations. Long-term consequences of deprivation include separation anxiety — fear of being abandoned by an attachment figure resulting in increased clinginess and stress. For adults, separation anxiety may cause insecurity and lack of trust.

Study: Belsky (1988)

Belsky analysed the combined results of several studies into the effects of daycare on attachment. The results suggested that attachment is negatively affected if a child spends more than 20 hours a week in non-maternal care.

Examiner tip

It is useful to know about more than one way of measuring attachment, then you can gain evaluation marks by comparing one method with another.

Knowledge check 3

Distinguish between privation and deprivation.

Romanian orphan studies and the effects of institutionalisation

Large numbers of Romanian children were found to be suffering extreme privation in orphanages in the 1990s. Many were adopted in the UK and they have been studied by the English and Romanian Adoptees (ERA) study team.

Age-related benefits of adoption

Rutter et al. (1998) compared Romanian orphans adopted in the UK with a control group of British adopted children. Four years after adoption there were no significant differences between the two groups in physical and cognitive development. However, the greatest 'catch-up' was seen in those who had arrived in Britain before 6 months of age.

Other ERA findings indicate that the consequences for children adopted after 6 months are not so positive. The Romanian institution-reared adoptees showed more autistic-like symptoms and unusual attachment behaviours than the UK controls. Beckett et al. (2006) found that many Romanian children aged over 6 months at the time of adoption continued to show negative cognitive effects at 11 years.

Evaluation

- Rutter's original view that the effects of privation can be overcome may be over-optimistic. For adoption after 6 months, the consequences seem long-lasting.
- The ERA research is large scale and well controlled. Previous work involved single cases or animal experiments.
- Negative effects may not be due to institutionalisation alone, but due to a severely impoverished and unstimulating environment.

Examiner tip

It is important to recognise that the Romanian orphan research is longitudinal and to try to present some of the more recent findings in an answer.

Bowlby's theory of attachment

Bowlby stated that mother love in infancy is just as important for a child's mental health as are vitamins and minerals for physical health. He suggested that young children need 'a warm, intimate and continuous relationship with mother'.

Main points

- Infants have an innate need to attach to one figure — **monotropy**.
- Young children need the continuous care of this person for the first 2 years — a critical period.
- Breaking of the attachment bond in the critical period results in irreversible long-term damage to the child.
- The consequences of maternal deprivation include delinquency, affectionless behaviour and intellectual retardation.

monotropy a preference for a single attachment figure

Evidence

- Harlow's monkey study (see p. 8) supported the view that separation from the mother had long-term consequences.
- Lorenz's research with geese showed that attachment behaviour (following behaviour) is innate in other species.

- Goldfarb (1943) compared outcomes for children raised in an institution and children who had been fostered. The group that had spent 3 years in an institution scored less well on cognitive and emotional tests.
- Bowlby carried out retrospective interviews with 44 juvenile thieves, 14 of whom were described as affectionless psychopaths who showed no feelings for others. Bowlby found that most of the affectionless individuals were separated from their mother in the first 2 years. Bowlby concluded that maternal deprivation in childhood leads to delinquency and affectionless behaviour.

Evaluation

- Bowlby confused deprivation and privation.
- Delinquency is related to the causes and circumstances of separation (e.g. family trauma) and how the separation is handled (Rutter, 1981).
- Hodges and Tizard (1989) argued against the 2-year critical period. They showed that children adopted at 7 years could develop attachments.
- Some animal studies suggest that the effects of early deprivation are reversible (Suomi and Harlow, 1972).
- Freud and Dann (1951) found that effective substitute care could mediate the effects of early separation. ERA research suggests that 'catch-up' is possible if adoption occurs early enough.
- Schaffer and Emerson (1964) argued against monotropy. Their study of Scottish infants showed that multiple attachments are the norm.

The work of Schaffer

Schaffer and Emerson (1964) studied attachment in 60 Glaswegian infants. They proposed four stages of attachment development:

(1) the asocial stage (0–6 weeks) — babies do not differentiate much between people and objects

(2) the diffuse stage (6 weeks–6 months) — babies have no obviously preferred attachment figure

(3) the single attachment stage (7–12 months) — babies show a strong preference for one attachment figure, with fear of strangers

(4) the multiple attachment stage (over 12 months) — most children have up to five attachment figures by 18 months

Later relationships

Summary specification content

The development of friendship in childhood and adolescence. Age-related change in friendship. Sex differences in children's friendship.

Research into the causes and consequences of popularity and rejection.

Friendship in childhood and adolescence

According to Smith et al. (2003) friendship is 'a close relationship between two particular people, as indicated by their association together or their psychological attachment and trust'.

Examiner tip

Any discussion of Bowlby's work should include evidence in favour of and against his theory. It is also important to discuss the implications of his work e.g. how child-care policy and practices have been affected by his theory.

Knowledge check 4

In what way did the work of Schaffer and Emerson contradict Bowlby's theory?

Examiner tip

Be careful not to base your answer just on personal experience. It should be founded in psychological theory and research. Do not write about your own friendships; instead refer to theory and evidence.

Age-related change in friendship

Most research focuses on changes in the understanding of friendship with age. Selman (1980) suggested five stages of friendship understanding:

(1) 3–6 years — physical partner
(2) 5–9 years — one-way assistant
(3) 7–12 years — reciprocity
(4) 10–15 years — exclusive intimacy
(5) over 12 years — autonomous interdependence

Study: Damon (1977)

Damon asked children questions about friendship. Under the age of 7 years, friendship is about who you play with. At 8–11 years, friendship is about shared interests, trust and kindness. From 12 years, friendship is about mutual understanding and intimacy. Damon concluded that understanding of friendship changes with age as children become less egocentric.

Study: Bigelow and La Gaipa (1975)

Bigelow and La Gaipa studied children's 'my best friend' stories. Younger children's stories focused on living close, play and common interests, whereas older children referred more to loyalty and intimacy. The researchers concluded that, as children get older, there is less emphasis on physical interaction and more focus on psychological characteristics and concern for others.

Evaluation

- Language ability may be a confounding variable. Older children can express complex emotional ideas more easily than younger children.
- Categorisation of dilemma responses/content of stories may be subjective.
- Hypothetical dilemma responses may not reflect real-life reasoning.

Sex differences in children's friendship

Relationships between boys are extensive — boys spend time in a large group and focus on shared activities. Relationships between girls are intensive — girls have intimate friendships in pairs and focus on emotional closeness. These differences continue into adolescence. Benenson and Christakos (2003) found that among 10–15-year-olds, girls had more 'best friends', boys' friendships lasted longer and girls worried more about friendship.

Study: Benenson (1990)

Benenson interviewed 10-year-olds and used rating scales to determine important aspects of friendship. The boys' data revealed friendships of large interconnected groups, with the focus on the status of the group. The girls' data revealed more intimate friendships or 'cliques'. Benenson concluded that social networks are different for boys and girls.

Knowledge check 5

Use your knowledge of research methods to suggest how Bigelow and La Gaipa could have analysed the data from the 'best friend' stories.

Examiner tip

It is often difficult to find things to discuss on sex differences in friendships. One option is to discuss psychological explanations for sex differences e.g. male/female hormones, evolutionary pressures, operant conditioning and social learning and modelling.

Study: Lever (1976)

Lever interviewed 10-year-old US boys and girls about their friendships. Girls preferred a best friend, were happy to show affection and shared intimate secrets. They were also more anxious about threats to friendships and more likely to be jealous. Boys' friendships were more open and more group-focused.

Popularity and rejection

sociometry a technique to represent relationships between members of a group in the form of a diagram (sociogram) that illustrates the popularity status of members of the group

Coie and Dodge (1983) used a method known as **sociometry** to identify five types of child: popular, average, controversial, neglected and rejected. Rejected children can be divided into two types (Berk, 2003):

- rejected-aggressive — impulsive, aggressive, hyperactive and lacking in ability to understand others
- rejected-withdrawn — passive, socially withdrawn, high in social anxiety and often targeted for bullying

Causes

- Similarity. Children choose friends who are similar in terms of sex, age, background etc. Unusual/deviant children tend to be excluded. Kandel (1978) found that friendships lasted longer if the friends were similar.
- Attractiveness. Children prefer attractive peers, with the effect more marked in girls than boys (Vaughn and Langlois, 1983). Attractiveness may be physical or linked to status.
- Personality. Rejected children are aggressive and disruptive. Dodge (1983) found a link between personality traits and popularity.
- Early relationships. According to the internal working model, the earliest bond between child and carer acts as a model for future relationships.
- Poor social skills.

Knowledge check 6

Dodge et al. carried out their observation in a playground. What type of observation was it? Give one strength and one limitation of this type of observation.

Study: Dodge et al. (1983)

Dodge et al. observed playground behaviour, watching a third child trying to join in with a pair already playing together. Popular children were socially adept and able to join in. Neglected children did not attempt to join in and rejected children were too aggressive and forceful.

Evaluation

- A clear cause-and-effect relationship cannot easily be established. Rejection may cause aggression rather than the other way round.
- Learning social skills can help avoid rejection (Oden and Asher, 1977).

Consequences

Rejected children are more likely to have psychiatric problems as adults (Cowen et al., 1973), experience alcoholism (Duck, 1991) and get into trouble with the law (Kuperschmidt and Coie, 1990).

Evaluation

- A cause-and-effect relationship between rejection and negative consequences cannot be determined.
- Schaffer (1996) suggests that aggressiveness may be the key factor rather than rejection.
- Most studies fail to distinguish between rejection and friendlessness. Bagwell et al. (1998) argued that rejection by some is less damaging than total friendlessness.

- Infant–caregiver interactions: imitation, interactional synchrony, physical contact, modified language, sensitive responsiveness.
- Functions of attachment: cupboard love theory (food), survival, communication and the internal working model.
- Harlow (1959) concluded attachment depends on comfort and privation leads to antisocial behaviour.
- Measures of attachment are: Strange Situation, Adult Attachment Interview, Attachment Q-sort.
- Ainsworth's three attachment types: secure, anxious-avoidant and anxious-resistant.
- Privation — never having had an attachment (Genie, Koluchova twins, Romanian orphans).
- Deprivation — when an attachment is disrupted/broken (Robertson studies).
- Short-term effect of deprivation — anger, despair, detachment. Long-term effects include separation anxiety.

- Early Romanian orphan research showed recovery. Later findings are less positive.
- Bowlby argued for innate, instinctual monotropy in the critical period and irreversible negative consequences, including delinquency and affectionless psychopathy.
- Schaffer proposed multiple attachments.
- Age-related changes in friendship shift from shared activities to intimacy and reciprocity.
- Boys' friendships are extensive, girls' are intensive.
- Coie and Dodge identified five types of child: popular, average, controversial, neglected, rejected.
- Causes of popularity/rejection include: similarity, attractiveness, aggression, internal working model, social skill.
- Consequences of rejection include psychiatric problems, alcoholism, deviance.

Summary

Cognitive development

Piaget's theory of cognitive development

Summary specification content

Schemas: adaptation, assimilation and accommodation. Piaget's stages of intellectual development. Characteristics of these stages, including object permanence, conservation, egocentrism, class inclusion. Piaget's research, including the three mountains experiment and conservation experiments.

Schemas, adaptation, assimilation and accommodation

A schema is a unit of knowledge. Piaget proposed that babies are born with simple schemas, for example sucking and grasping schemas. Infants soon develop new schemas, such as throwing schemas.

Examiner tip

Make sure you can define Piaget's terms clearly and have concrete examples of schema development. For example, you could explain the process whereby a grip schema for holding a crayon is adapted as the child moves on to using a smaller pencil.

The process of developing schemas in response to experience of the world is called adaptation. Adaptation occurs through two processes:

(1) assimilation — adding to an existing schema or applying an existing schema to a new situation

(2) accommodation — altering a schema or developing a new schema to cope with a new situation

Piaget referred to disequilibrium, which is a state of cognitive imbalance that is experienced when what we know about the world is inconsistent with incoming information. Cognitive balance or equilibrium is restored through accommodation. Piaget was a constructivist: he believed that understanding of the world is constructed through experience and discovery. He thought that children learned through active discovery and his theory of discovery learning was influential in primary education.

Piaget's stages of intellectual development and his research

Piaget proposed four invariant and universal stages of cognitive development. The child's understanding is different at each stage:

(1) 0–2 years — the sensori-motor stage

(2) 2–7 years — the pre-operational stage

(3) 7–12 years — the concrete operational stage

(4) over 12 years — the formal operational stage

The sensori-motor stage

Knowledge is limited to simple motor reflexes and sensations. There is no object concept — the child has no awareness of objects outside the immediate present. Early in the sensori-motor stage there is no distinction between self and others. Intentional behaviour begins at about 8 months and by the end of this stage general symbolic function is acquired, so the child understands that one thing can stand for another. Object permanence (object concept) arises at around 8 months.

object permanence (object concept) the understanding that objects continue to exist even when they are out of sight

Study: Piaget (1963)

Piaget tested object permanence by taking a toy from the child and hiding it under a blanket. Before 8 months of age, infants would not reach for the hidden toy. Infants over 8 months would search for the toy, showing that they had object permanence. Piaget concluded that object permanence develops at around 8 months.

Evaluation

- Failure to reach for the toy may not mean that the infants did not understand that it still existed: they might have thought that it was not allowed, or have lacked motor skills.
- Other studies showed that even 3-month-old babies have object permanence. Bower and Wishart (1972) turned out the lights and found that infants continued to reach for an object in the dark.

Knowledge check 7

Why might the infants in the Bower and Wishart study have shown object permanence whereas the infants in the Piaget study did not?

The pre-operational stage

Pre-operational children cannot perform many cognitive tasks. They cannot perform logical operations (mental tasks). This stage is sometimes divided into two sub-stages: the pre-conceptual (2–4 years) and the intuitive (4–7 years). Typical thinking errors include animism (attributing feelings to inanimate objects), centration (the ability to think about only one feature at a time) and egocentrism. Piaget's three mountains experiment illustrates egocentrism.

egocentrism the inability to think about something from another person's point of view

Study: Piaget and Inhelder (1956)

Piaget and Inhelder showed 4–12-year-olds a model of three mountains. A doll was placed somewhere on the model. From the other side of the model the child had to choose the view that the doll would be able to see. Children aged 4–5 years chose their own view but by 7–8 years they could choose the correct view. Piaget concluded that pre-operational children cannot decentre: they are egocentric.

Examiner tip
Descriptions of the three mountains experiment should be accurate. Explain how participants were asked to choose the doll's view from a series of 10 pictures.

Study: Hughes (1978)

Hughes showed 3½–5-year-olds a model with intersecting walls. A boy doll and a policeman doll were positioned in the model and the child had to say if the policeman could see the boy. They then had to hide the boy doll from the policeman doll. Hughes found that 90% of children were successful.

Evaluation

- The three-mountains task was unrealistic. Borke's (1975) child-friendly version used television characters and even three- or four-year-olds could give the correct answer.
- Piaget underestimated children's ability. Hughes showed that decentring occurs sooner than Piaget had thought.

Conservation is the ability to understand that the properties of objects or materials stay the same, even though outward appearance may change. This occurs because thinking is ruled by appearance. Piaget's **conservation experiments** involved volume, mass and number.

Study: Piaget and Szeminska (1941)

Piaget and Szeminska showed children two identical containers, each holding the same amount of liquid. They asked each child individually whether there was the same amount in each container or whether one had more. They then poured the liquid from one container into a different tall, thin container. The same question was asked again (post-transformation question). Most children under 7 years replied that the tall, thin container had more liquid. The over-7-year-olds gave the correct answer. It seems that the ability to conserve arises at around 7 years.

Examiner tip
When describing conservation studies, it is important to make it clear that the materials were somehow transformed and the same question was asked again.

Evaluation

- The use of the word 'more' may have confused the children. Perhaps they think of 'more' as 'higher' or 'fuller'.
- Asking the same question twice was confusing. Children might have given a different answer the second time because they thought that the first answer was wrong. Rose and Blank (1974) omitted the first question and found 6-year-olds performed better. McGarrigle and Donaldson's (1974) version with Naughty Teddy showed 60% of 6-year-olds could conserve if the rearrangement of the materials (beads) appeared to be accidental.
- The original studies have been described as lacking 'human sense'.

The concrete operational stage

At 7 years old the child starts to perform mental operations (logical thinking) and is able to conserve. One operation is reversibility — the ability to mentally reverse actions. At this stage, logical thinking is limited to concrete problems. The child can perform conservation and class inclusion tasks.

Study: Piaget and Szeminska (1941)

Piaget and Szeminska tested understanding of overall classes and sub-classes using 20 wooden beads (18 brown and 2 white). Children were asked three questions: Are the beads all wooden? Are there more brown beads or more white beads? Are there more brown beads or more wooden beads? Children under 7 years answered the third question incorrectly, whereas over 7 years they answered it correctly because they could distinguish between the overall class (beads) and the sub-class (brown beads).

Evaluation

- The class inclusion questions are unusual and confusing.
- Making the question more accessible produced different results. In McGarrigle's cow version, 48% of 6-year-olds could complete the task.

The formal operational stage

Children can now think **abstractly** and **hypothetically**. Formal operational thought is more **flexible** than concrete operational thought. Formal operational thinkers can use **hypothetico-deductive reasoning** and **systematic hypothesis testing**.

Study: Inhelder and Piaget (1958)

Inhelder and Piaget used the pendulum problem to test formal operational reasoning. They found that formal operational thinkers varied each factor systematically, changing one variable at a time and enabling them to correctly conclude which factors affected the rate of the pendulum swing.

class inclusion
understanding the relationship between an overall category and sub-categories

Knowledge check 8

Identify three types of task that children cannot usually perform until they reach the concrete operational stage.

Examiner tip

Focus on the question set and do not provide overlong descriptions of the whole theory, including all the stages and every experimental study. Poorly focused answers tend to get few marks. Look carefully at the question. Is it asking you about specific stages or abilities? If so, limit your answer to the relevant information.

Evaluation of Piaget's theory and methods

- Piaget's stages were too rigid. He later proposed 'horizontal décalage', where a child may straddle more than one stage.
- His sequence of development has been confirmed in several cultures, although children from non-industrialised societies reach the stages later.
- Not all adults demonstrate formal operational thinking.
- Discovery learning may not be sufficient: Vygotsky argued that guidance is essential.
- The sample was small, his records lacked detail and the research was not strictly controlled.
- The tasks were confusing and Piaget assumed that a lack of success meant a lack of ability.
- Gelman (1969) found that conservation was almost impossible to teach, supporting Piaget's ideas about readiness.
- Piaget's child-centred approach had a huge effect on education.
- The clinical interview method yielded rich qualitative information, which stimulated much research.

Alternative approaches to children's cognition

Summary specification content

Vygotsky and cognitive development within a social and cultural context. Vygotsky's zone of proximal development. Scaffolding. Guided participation in sociocultural activity.

Nativist explanations and early infant abilities, including knowledge of the physical world (Baillargeon).

The information processing approach: Seigler's research into problem-solving strategies.

Vygotsky and cognitive development

Vygotsky's theory was sociocultural. He said that cognitive development was influenced by the social world and culture. Vygotsky thought that children needed to develop the cognitive tools (e.g. language, number systems) of their culture. He proposed that children internalise the knowledge of others and learn through social experiences. He saw the child as an apprentice.

Zone of proximal development

The zone of proximal development (ZPD) is the difference or distance between what a child can do alone and what he or she can achieve with help. The ZPD considers potential, not just current ability.

Study: Hedegaard (1996)

Hedegaard used a special teaching method to extend children's abilities through their ZPD. Learning activities were designed on three interrelated topics. The children had to integrate the different sets of information to answer questions. Careful structuring of activities enabled whole-class groups of children to work towards their individual potential and through their ZPD.

Knowledge check 9

Suggest three ways in which Piaget's views might have affected primary education.

readiness Piaget's view that children could not be made to understand new concepts until they were cognitively ready, suggesting that cognitive development cannot be accelerated.

Knowledge check 10

What did Vygotsky mean when he referred to the child as 'an apprentice' who learns through 'internalisation'?

Scaffolding

Scaffolding involves help and support from an adult or more able peer. Help is gradually withdrawn until the child is independently competent. Scaffolding can occur in many contexts with parents, siblings, older peers and teachers. It has been found to occur in many cultures.

Study: Wood and Middleton (1975)

Wood and Middleton observed parents helping young children build bricks. The task was too hard for the children to do alone. Parents initially showed their child, then stopped giving direct help but made comments and suggestions. The amount of help was reduced over time.

Evaluation

- This study shows scaffolding of a specific task but this does not show that scaffolding occurs with more general understanding, for example of concepts.

Guided participation in sociocultural activity

Scaffolding of cultural traditions and practices is known as guided participation (Rogoff et al., 1995). Adults model an activity and guide the child in his or her efforts. The child finally reconstructs the knowledge and adopts his or her own version. Rogoff believed that cognitive development is dependent on environment and culture.

Study: Rogoff (1995)

Rogoff studied the transmission of knowledge in the annual Girl Scout Cookie Sale in the USA. More experienced members of the community passed on knowledge of the event and gave advice and practical help. This knowledge was then reformulated as the girls found new ways of working.

Language

Vygotsky believed that language was a key factor in cognitive development. He stated that monologues enabled a child to plan behaviour. At first these are out loud, then, at around the age of 7, they become internalised (i.e. thought).

Evaluation

- Vygotsky's theory suggests acceleration of cognitive development is possible. Some studies show acceleration is difficult (Gelman, 1969).
- Adult instruction can sometimes be confusing and too much instruction may result in a lack of initiative.
- Vygotsky's ideas have educational applications (e.g. peer tutoring, collective argumentation, community of inquiry).

Examiner tip
Make sure you can give everyday examples of guided participation in a sociocultural activity, for example, preparing for a party. Your example should make it clear who is doing the guiding of whom (e.g. father shows son) and the specific behaviour (how to offer crisps to guests).

Examiner tip
Be able to describe classroom applications of Vygotsky's theory.

Study: Elbers and Streefland (2000)

Elbers and Streefland tested the effectiveness of a community of inquiry in a Dutch school. Teachers and pupils played the role of researcher during maths activities. Teachers gave no explicit instruction but simply rephrased children's comments, correcting errors. The children cooperated well, used evidence constructively and were highly productive.

Nativist explanations and early infant abilities

Nativists believe we are born with innate structures determining cognitive ability and that developmental change is due to genetic predisposition. This contrasts with Piaget's constructivist view of cognitive development as a result of active experience.

nativism a philosophical view that states that human characteristics are innate or inborn

Knowledge of the physical world

Certain abilities such as depth perception may be innate. Bower et al. (1970) found that young infants could perceive an object looming towards them. Gibson and Walk (1960) found that babies aged 6–14 months could perceive depth in a 'visual cliff' experiment.

constructivism the view that knowledge of the world is built up (constructed) on the basis of experience

Baillargeon challenged Piaget's views on object permanence. She devised experiments where infants were presented with impossible events. If children showed surprise, this suggested that they had a mental representation of what ought to occur and had object permanence. One study involved a truck rolling down a slope; the other involved a carrot passing behind a screen. In the truck study, Baillargeon found that 6–8-month-olds showed object permanence.

Study: Baillargeon (1991)

Three-month-old babies watched tall and short carrots move from left to right behind a screen. They then saw the same procedure with a screen that had a window in the top half. The tall carrot should have been visible in the window but the researchers made the event 'impossible', with the tall carrot not visible in the window. Babies looked longer in the tall-carrot condition than the short-carrot condition, showing they had object permanence.

Examiner tip

The impossible event experiments carried out by Baillargeon are sometimes referred to as 'violation of expectation' studies because the child does not see what he or she expects to see.

Evaluation

- Baillargeon's studies contradict Piaget's views and possibly support a nativist view.

Knowledge check 11

What did Baillargeon's impossible event studies show?

The information processing approach

According to this approach, human processing is like the processing of a computer. Research is concentrated on individual cognitive processes. Information processing theorists believe that age-related changes are due to increased cognitive efficiency. Bee (1997) suggests that with age there is greater processing efficiency and capacity, the development of rules and the development of metacognition (an awareness of one's own cognitive abilities).

Study: Flavell et al. (1996)

Flavell et al. investigated memory strategies used by children aged 5–10 years. Few of the younger children used the strategy of verbal repetition when told to remember pictures. In contrast, most of the older children used this strategy. Flavell concluded that information processing strategies change with age.

Siegler's research into problem-solving strategies

Siegler (1976) proposed that cognitive development involves the acquisition of rules or strategies for solving problems. With age these rules become more complex and can be applied to different problems.

Study: Siegler (1976)

Siegler used a balance scale task with 5–17-year-olds to find out if information processing strategies changed as children got older. On each trial different weights were positioned at different places on a fulcrum. The child had to predict whether the scale would tip and, if so, which way. Before the trials Siegler identified four increasingly complex strategies. Children used the more complex (and successful) strategies as they got older.

Siegler (1996) proposed that problem-solving strategies overlap and children choose which strategy to use at any one time. The overlapping waves theory has been used in computer simulations of developing cognitive processes.

Evaluation of the information processing approach

- Information processing findings can inform new teaching techniques.
- Information processing findings can be linked to biological research into brain function.
- The view is not as comprehensive as Piaget's theory of cognitive development.

Comparing Piaget with alternative approaches

Table 2 Comparing Piaget's theory

Piaget	Vygotsky
Cognitive development depends on self-discovery	Cognitive development depends on guidance and support from others
Knowledge develops through an inbuilt tendency to adaptation — child is a 'lone scientist'	Knowledge develops through sociocultural interaction — child is an 'apprentice' to more experienced peers
Sees language as incidental or a by-product of cognitive development	Sees language as critical for cognitive development
Increased understanding occurs when child is ready (the readiness approach) and cannot be accelerated	Cognitive understanding can be increased and accelerated through instruction and guidance

Examiner tip

It is not really correct to say that Siegler ignored the role of social factors in cognitive development. Siegler found that participants given feedback from another person learned complex problem-solving strategies more quickly, suggesting that social interaction is important as well as age.

Knowledge check 12

What did Siegler mean when he referred to 'overlapping waves'?

Examiner tip

You should be able to compare theories, for example compare Piaget's theory with the alternative approaches (Table 2).

- Piaget: schemas develop though assimilation and accommodation.
- Piaget proposed four stages of cognitive development: sensori-motor; pre-operational; concrete operational; formal operational.
- Object permanence develops during the sensori-motor stage.
- Pre-operational children are egocentric.
- Conservation, class inclusion and decentring develop by the concrete operational stage.
- The three-mountains experiment shows egocentrism.
- Conservation is understanding that properties of objects remain the same despite changes in outside appearance.
- Vygotsky emphasised the role of sociocultural factors, arguing children internalise the world view of others — the child as an apprentice.

- The ZPD: distance between what a child can do alone and with help.
- Scaffolding: the child is supported and the support is gradually withdrawn.
- Guided participation (Rogoff): scaffolding of a socio-cultural activity.
- Nativism: belief that cognitive abilities are innate.
- Baillargeon's impossible event experiments show understanding of the physical world.
- The information processing approach emphasises increased cognitive efficiency and problem-solving strategies.
- Siegler's balance scale test showed four stages of problem solving and showed strategies can overlap.

Moral development

Piaget and Kohlberg

Summary specification content

Piaget's stages of moral development: pre-moral judgement, moral realism and moral relativism. Kohlberg's pre-conventional, conventional and post-conventional levels. The stages within these levels.

Ways of investigating moral development including the use of moral comparisons and moral dilemmas.

Piaget's stages of moral development

The pre-moral stage

Under 5 years of age the child cannot make sensible moral judgements.

The moral realism stage

Between 5 and 9 years of age, moral judgements are based on other's views of right and wrong (heteronomous) and on consequences rather than intention. Rules are seen as inflexible moral absolutes. Right and wrong are seen as objective reality rather than opinion and there is a belief that wrongdoing should be heavily punished (expiatory punishment). Unpleasant events that occur after wrongdoing are seen as punishments (immanent justice).

The moral relativism stage

Over 10 years of age, judgement is based on an internalised moral code (**autonomous**). Both intention and consequence are relevant. Rules are no longer seen as fixed, but can be changed. Moral judgement is seen to be a matter of subjective opinion and punishment should be **reciprocal** (reflect the nature of the crime)

Piaget thought that progress through these three stages depended on (a) declining egocentrism (allowing for the taking of other people's perspectives) and (b) the ability to decentre (allowing for the consideration of several issues at a time).

Evaluation

- Evidence suggests that older children focus more on intention than younger children (Berk, 2003).
- Piaget's theory assumes that moral understanding is fixed at 10 years, but others suggest it continues to develop into adulthood.
- Even adults judge by consequence rather than by intention on occasions.
- The findings were based on research with a limited sample.
- Piaget underestimated children's ability. Nelson (1980) and Helwig et al. (2001) found that 3-year-olds could consider intention.

Piaget's moral comparisons

Children heard two separate stories. In one story, a boy causes a lot of damage by accident (breaks 15 cups). In another story, a boy causes a small amount of intentional damage (breaks one cup). Piaget asked which boy was naughtier and why. He found that children aged under 10 years thought that the boy in the story with more damage was naughtier, whereas children aged 10 years and over considered the intention.

Evaluation

- The moral comparison task places great demand on memory.
- The stories manipulate two variables at once. Nelson (1980) systematically varied the extent of damage and the intention. Where intention was clear, even three-year-olds considered both intention and consequence.

Piaget's work on telling lies

Piaget found that younger children thought that 'big', absurd lies were naughtier than 'small' lies involving less distortion from the truth. He found older children considered not just whether the statement is false, but also intent to deceive.

Piaget's work on understanding of rules

Piaget (1932) watched children playing marbles and asked them about the rules. Children aged 4–5 did not seem to understand the rules; at 6–9 years they could follow rules but sometimes cheated — they believed that rules were fixed by a higher authority. By 10 years they understood that the rules could be changed by common consent.

Knowledge check 13

Outline two differences between moral realism and moral relativism.

Examiner tip

In a discussion of Piaget's theory of moral development it is useful to analyse why children's reasoning changes and explain how lessening egocentrism affects the understanding of right and wrong, telling lies and understanding of rules.

Kohlberg's theory of moral development and the moral dilemma technique

Kohlberg (1969) extended Piaget's work. He used the moral dilemma technique in which the participant hears a story about a person faced with a choice between two courses of action, each in some way immoral. The most famous was the 'Heinz' dilemma. Heinz has to choose between stealing a drug to save his dying wife and not stealing the drug, thereby allowing her to die. After listening to the story, participants were asked a series of questions in a structured interview. Verbal responses were categorised according to stage of moral reasoning.

Study: Kohlberg (1963)

Kohlberg used the dilemma technique with 72 boys. They were interviewed every 3 years for 20 years (Colby et al., 1983). Younger boys reasoned on the basis of possible punishment, whereas older boys reasoned on the basis of care, the law and opinions of society. Kohlberg concluded that moral reasoning becomes more complex with age and that it develops in six stages.

Study: Walker et al. (1987)

Walker et al. compared hypothetical and real-life moral reasoning. Adults and children were interviewed about three of Kohlberg's dilemmas and one real-life personal dilemma. Most participants were at the same stage of moral reasoning for the hypothetical and real-life dilemmas. Walker concluded that hypothetical dilemma responses reflect real-life moral reasoning.

Knowledge check 14

What is the difference between the moral comparison technique and the moral dilemma technique?

Evaluation

- Dilemmas may be too difficult.
- The situations are not real-life, so the technique lacks validity.
- The technique may not have predictive validity, although Kohlberg (1975) found consistency increased between hypothetical and real-life reasoning as people progressed up the stages.
- The technique may be measuring education rather than moral reasoning.
- Analysis may be subjective. However, Kohlberg established high inter-rater reliability using detailed instructions.

Kohlberg's levels and stages of moral reasoning

According to Kohlberg, the six-stage sequence is invariant and irreversible

Examiner tip
Be careful not to confuse Kohlberg's levels and stages.

The pre-conventional level

(1) Punishment stage — reasoning is based on whether or not an action would be punished.
(2) Reward stage — reasoning is based on whatever benefits the individual (instrumental gain).

The conventional level

(3) Good-boy, good-girl stage — judgements are based on what other people would approve or disapprove of.

(4) Law and order stage — moral choices reflect obedience to authority and adherence to the law.

The post-conventional level

(5) Social contract stage — decisions involve the consideration of unique circumstances and basic human rights. There is recognition that laws are not always fair.

(6) Ethical principle stage — decisions are governed by self-chosen ethical principles that are seen to be more important than the law.

Study: Walker (1989)

Walker investigated Kohlberg's theory of an invariant and irreversible sequence of development. Participants were tested using dilemmas over 2 years. The responses were scored and categorised according to Kohlberg's stages. Over the 2 years, 37% of participants moved to the next stage, 6% regressed and none skipped a stage.

Evaluation

- Turiel (1978) criticised the distinct stages, proposing different moral domains with moral reasoning differing according to the domain.
- Stage 6 was abandoned in 1975.
- Moral reasoning may not tally with behaviour (Hartshorne and May, 1928).
- Cross-cultural work generally supports Kohlberg's stage sequence (Berk, 2003), although the scoring system may reflect Western values.
- Gilligan (1982) thought that Kohlberg neglected female moral development. She suggested women's answers were more empathic (stage 3), whereas men's answers focused on rights and law (stage 4).
- Walker et al. (1987) found no sex differences using Kohlberg's scoring system.

Knowledge check 15

Why is Kohlberg's second level referred to as the 'conventional' level?

Alternatives to Piaget and Kohlberg

Summary specification content

Eisenberg's model of pro-social reasoning, including hedonistic, needs, approval, self-reflective and internalised orientations.

Gilligan's ethic of care: differences between boys and girls. Gilligan's three levels of moral development.

Damon's research into distributive justice.

Psychodynamic explanations of moral development. The role of the superego.

AQA(B) A2 Psychology

Eisenberg's model of pro-social reasoning

Eisenberg (1983) used pro-social dilemmas, for example the 'birthday party' dilemma.

Study: Eisenberg et al. (1987)

In a longitudinal study, Eisenberg et al. interviewed children aged between 4 and 12 years about pro-social dilemmas. Pre-school and nursery children were hedonistic (put their own interests and pleasures before the needs of others). Older children were empathic (focused on the feelings of others).

Eisenberg proposed five levels, similar to Kohlberg's stages:

(1) hedonistic — correct action is that which benefits self
(2) needs-oriented — correct action is that which considers others' needs
(3) approval-oriented — correct action is that which would be approved of
(4) self-reflective (empathic) — correct action involves sympathy and role-taking
(5) strongly internalised — correct action is based on clear values of dignity and respect

Evaluation

- The pattern of change parallels Kohlberg.
- Pro-social reasoning is often more advanced than reasoning about wrongdoing.
- Eisenberg was the first to consider pro-social reasoning.
- Some cross-cultural evidence confirms the levels (Boehnke et al., 1989).

Gilligan's ethic of care: differences between boys and girls

Gilligan (1982) argued that Kohlberg placed more importance on justice-based reasoning than on care-based reasoning and was biased in favour of males. She also criticised Kohlberg's use of male participants. Gilligan said that women's reasoning is as complex as men's, but different; women focus on relationships and care (morality of care) and men focus on rights and law (morality of justice):

- morality of care — concern about the effect of actions on the feelings and needs of others
- morality of justice — concern about whether or not rules have been broken and appropriate punishment

Study: Gilligan (1977)

Gilligan used unstructured interviews with 29 women considering abortion. She found they focused on responsibility and feelings (Kohlberg's stage 3) rather than justice. She therefore proposed three levels of female morality.

Gilligan's three levels of moral development

(1) **self-interest** — focus on what is best for self
(2) **self-sacrifice** — focus on the welfare of others rather than one's own needs
(3) **non-violence or universal care** — focus on the importance of not hurting others

hedonistic pleasure-seeking

Examiner tip

Descriptions of Eisenberg's theory should focus on moral reasoning. Eisenberg tested what children thought and said about helping others. She did not test how they actually behaved.

Examiner tip

Discussion can be expanded here. Sex differences in moral reasoning proposed by Gilligan can be linked to psychodynamic theory about identification and gender: a boy internalises his father's views about justice and fairness and a girl internalises her mother's views about care and helping.

Study: Walker (1989)

Walker tested people on hypothetical and real-life dilemmas, scoring responses using both Kohlberg's stages and Gilligan's levels. Both male and female participants were found to use care-based and justice-based orientations. This study confirmed that there were no substantial sex differences in moral reasoning.

Knowledge check 16

Why might Gilligan's work be said to have greater validity than most other research into moral development?

Evaluation

- The kind of reasoning may depend more on the type of dilemma than on the sex of the participant (Walker, 1989).
- Gilligan interviewed only women. Men may have used similar arguments in their reasoning about abortion.

Damon's research into distributive justice

Damon (1977) studied reasoning about how things should be fairly divided (distributive justice) and found it became more sophisticated with age. Young children reason on the basis of personal gain. At around 5 years, there is a fixed idea of equality, ignoring differences in effort. By 7 years, reasoning is based on merit. By 8–9 years, reasoning is based on benevolence, with special consideration for the disadvantaged.

Study: Damon (1977)

Damon asked children aged 4–10 years how they would share money from a picture sale. The youngest children thought that they should have the most. The 5–7-year-olds wanted to share the profit equally. Over 7 years they considered individual effort and need. Damon concluded that distributive justice shifts from focus on self to focus on fairness and others.

Knowledge check 17

How does Damon's research differ from the research into morality carried out by other researchers?

Evaluation

- Damon offered a different view on moral development.
- Findings generally reflect changes observed by Kohlberg and Eisenberg.
- Cross-cultural findings support Damon's results.
- The distributive justice dilemmas are realistic for children.

Psychodynamic explanations of moral development

Psychodynamic theory focuses on the emotional aspect of morality. Freud (1923) thought that morality is acquired in the phallic stage of psychosexual development at around 4–6 years.

The role of the superego

Freud proposed three parts to the personality: id, ego and superego. The superego is responsible for morality. It develops through the resolution of the Oedipus/Electra complex in the phallic stage. It acts as an internal parent or conscience, punishing

Examiner tip

There should be focus on aspects of Freud's theory that relate to moral development. Too much general Freudian theory would result in a largely irrelevant answer.

us with guilt if we behave badly. It also includes the ego-ideal, which indicates high moral standards. The superego represents the parent's values and standards.

The Oedipus complex

At 5 years of age the boy desires his mother and fears castration by his father. To resolve the conflict the boy gives up the desire for the mother and identifies with the father (the aggressor), internalising the father's moral values (the superego).

The Electra complex

Believing she has already been castrated, the girl identifies with the mother, internalising her moral values (the superego). According to Freud, females do not identify as strongly as males because girls are less afraid than boys. Freud therefore believed that women are morally inferior.

Evaluation

- There is no evidence that the superego exists.
- Children understand right and wrong before 5 years of age (Nelson, 1980) and moral reasoning continues to develop after 5 years.
- The view of women as morally inferior is not supported (Hoffman, 1975).
- Children without a same-sex parent do not appear to be any less moral.
- According to social learning theory, moral behaviour is influenced by peers, role models etc. and not just the same-sex parent.

Examiner tip

Any description of the psychodynamic explanation for moral development is incomplete unless you explain the role of 'identification' and 'internalisation'.

Knowledge check 18

According to which theories of moral development is moral reasoning in females less sophisticated than moral reasoning in males?

Summary

- Piaget proposed three stages of moral development: premoral; moral realism; moral relativism.
- Piaget's methods included: moral comparisons, interviews about lying, interviews about rules.
- Kohlberg proposed three levels and six stages: pre-conventional (punishment and reward); conventional (good-boy good-girl, and law and order); post-conventional (social contract and ethical principle).
- Kohlberg used the moral dilemma technique.

- Eisenberg studied pro-social reasoning: hedonistic, needs, approval, self-reflective, internalised stages. She used the Birthday Party dilemma.
- Gilligan focused on sex differences in moral reasoning: females — morality of care; males — morality of justice. Using abortion interviews, she proposed three levels: self-interest, self-sacrifice and non-violence/universal care.
- Damon studied distributive justice.
- Psychodynamic explanations focus on development of the superego.

Applied options

Cognition and law

Recognising and remembering faces

Summary specification content

Processes involved in recognition of faces. Explanations for face recognition, including feature analysis and holistic forms.

The construction of likenesses using composite systems.

Identification procedures: simultaneous and sequential line-ups.

Processes involved in recognition of faces

Identification is looking at a face and knowing who it is; recognition is knowing we have seen a face before; recall is describing (or drawing) a face from memory. Recognition is easier than identification.

Explanations for face recognition

Feature analysis theory

This is a bottom-up or data driven theory of information processing, which states that incoming visual cues (facial features) drive recognition. Some studies show features are important. Ellis et al. (1979) found that we rely more on external facial features such as hair and face shape to recognise less familiar people and internal features to recognise faces of more familiar people.

bottom-up theory
a theory that emphasises the importance of incoming visual cues for perception

Study: Woodhead et al. (1979)

Woodhead et al. studied the use of a training course in feature-based face recognition. Participants trained to recognise individual facial features were less able to identify a target face than controls, suggesting simple feature analysis is not so important for face recognition.

Examiner tip
It is not appropriate to conclude that face recognition is either bottom-up or top-down. In the end, it has to be a combination of bottom-up and top-down information that allows us to recognise faces.

Evaluation

- Basic bottom-up information (a face with features) is essential for recognition.
- Bottom-up processing is unlikely to explain face recognition completely: other factors such as expression are probably important.
- Individual features cannot be recognised out of context (Tanaka and Farah, 1993).
- Feature theory cannot explain why faces are harder to recognise if configuration is altered.

Holistic form theory

This is a top-down theory which states that previously stored semantic information is important for face recognition (Bruce and Young, 1986). We recognise a face as a whole, analysing not just features but also configuration, feelings and semantic information. For each face we have seen before, we have a stored template:

- stage 1: structural encoding — the visual structure of the face is analysed
- stage 2: face recognition unit (FRU) triggered, like a pattern or template
- stage 3: personal identity node (PIN) triggered, which includes semantic information about the person
- stage 4: name generation

Examiner tip

The four Bruce and Young stages need to be explained, not just named. Remember to say that it is a sequential theory: the stages occur in order.

Study: Young and Hay (1986)

Young and Hay showed participants some faces cut across horizontally, recording recognition times for each separate half. Two non-matching halves were put together to make a composite face and participants had to name the people in the two halves. Recognition time was greater when the two were in a composite that seemed to produce a completely new holistic face. This shows features are less important for recognition than wholes.

Other studies show how changing the layout leads to longer recognition time: Haig (1984) altered the spacing between features; Yin (1969) inverted faces.

Study: Tanaka and Farah (1993)

Tanaka and Farah showed how it was difficult to identify single features in isolation. Participants learned to recognise a face and could then tell if the face was presented with a different nose from the original. However, they could not distinguish between the original nose and the new nose when the noses were presented out of context (without the face), supporting the holistic theory.

Prosopagnosia and Capgras syndrome are disorders of face recognition. Both show that face recognition involves cognition and emotion, suggesting it may be holistic.

Study: Young et al. (1985)

Young et al. asked participants to keep a diary of face recognition events. Content analysis showed that people's recognition experiences confirmed Bruce and Young's four-stage sequence — no one reported being able to name someone without first knowing other things about them.

Knowledge check 19

Name the four stages of face recognition proposed by Bruce and Young.

Evaluation

- Evidence supports the Bruce and Young sequence and the importance of configuration.
- The theory acknowledges the role of emotion and semantic information.
- The theory has been elaborated using computer modelling (Burton et al., 1990).

Construction of likenesses using composite systems

composite system
a system of constructing a face from component parts

A composite system involves constructing a face from separate features (e.g. identikit, photo-fit, e-fit). First-generation systems were paper-based. Nowadays they are computerised, eliminating the obvious lines between features and allowing for feature blending and changes in spacing. Early systems were not always effective. Second-generation systems use computers to draw a composite based on verbal description, adding 'standard' features where there are gaps. Recent computerised systems are highly effective: EvoFIT uses six 'parent' faces that resemble the perpetrator. Features from these faces are then combined to 'breed' a second generation of faces for likenesses.

Study: Ellis et al. (1978)

Ellis et al. compared the accuracy of an early photo-fit system with hand-drawn sketches. Working from memory, the photo-fit system was more accurate than the sketch. However, with the target face present, the sketches were judged to be more accurate than photo-fits.

Evaluation

- Early systems were limited. New-generation systems are more effective (Davies et al., 2000).
- Kapardis (1997) found that the FACE system enabled confirmation of a suspect in 23% of cases.
- Studies lack ecological validity. In real life witnesses do not have time to study the face, and the person using the likeness to identify a suspect will probably know the suspect.

Identification procedures: simultaneous and sequential line-ups

simultaneous at the same time

UK identity parades usually involve a real suspect and eight 'foils'. In a simultaneous line-up, the witness sees all members of the line-up together. This may lead to a relative judgement about which person is most like the suspect. According to Wells et al. (1998), witnesses assume the suspect must be in the line-up and will choose someone even if they are unsure, increasing the chance of false identification. Malpass and Devine (1981) found that telling witnesses that a culprit may or may not be present significantly reduces false identifications.

sequential one after another

Lindsay and Wells (1985) introduced the sequential line-up, where possible suspects are seen one at a time and the witness has to make an absolute judgement about each.

Examiner tip
The Steblay study involved analysis of data from 30 different studies, a type of research known as meta-analysis. A discussion might consider the strengths/limitations of meta-analysis.

Study: Steblay et al. (2001)

Steblay et al. analysed 30 studies comparing simultaneous and sequential line-ups. They found that a suspect was more likely to be identified in simultaneous line-ups, even when the culprit was not actually present. In the most realistic studies, sequential line-ups resulted in a similar number of correct identifications and fewer false identifications.

Many line-ups now use a video system (e.g. the VIPER system — Kemp et al., 2001) where witnesses see a video sequence of the suspect among eight videos of foils. The VIPER system is sequential and highly controlled, and has legal equivalence with traditional line-ups.

Evaluation

- Sequential line-ups reduce the chance of false identifications.
- Video line-ups avoid problems of control.
- Other factors that affect identification procedures include similarity of foils, unintentional cues from the police officer, feedback.

Recalling events

Summary specification content

Factors affecting the reliability of eyewitness accounts and eyewitness identification, including post-event contamination. Improving eyewitness recall, including features of the cognitive interview. Children as eyewitnesses. Flashbulb memory: memory for shocking events.

The false memory debate. Controversy surrounding the recovery of repressed memories. The existence of false memories. Evidence relating to repression and false memory. Ethical and theoretical implications of the false memory debate.

Bartlett used the 'War of the Ghosts' study to show how recall involves 'effort after meaning', suggesting that memories are actively altered to fit with our existing schema; memory is active, reconstructive and can involve confabulation. This means that eyewitness identification is likely to be unreliable and for this reason courts are careful not to assume single eyewitness accounts are reliable (Devlin Report, 1976).

Factors affecting the reliability of eyewitness accounts

These include post-event contamination, emotion/stress, weapon focus, context and expectations/stereotypes.

Post-event contamination

This happens when a witness's memory of an event is altered after the event either by questioning or through discussion. Loftus et al. (1970s) found that leading questions influence recall. For example, Loftus and Palmer (1974) showed how changing the word 'smashed' and 'hit' in a question about a car crash led to differing estimates of speed (40.8 and 34 miles per hour).

Study: Loftus (1975)

Loftus showed participants a car accident on film and asked either 'How fast was the white sports car going when it passed the stop sign?' or 'How fast was the white sports car going when it passed the barn?' In the film there was a stop sign, but no barn. Significantly more participants reported seeing a barn in the second condition.

Knowledge check 20

What is meant by
(i) absolute judgement and
(ii) relative judgement?

confabulation where a memory is adjusted to fit with expectations, beliefs, stereotypes etc.

Examiner tip

Post-event contamination is the only named factor affecting reliability of EW accounts on the specification. However, if asked about factors, you ought to discuss more than one.

Another source of post-event contamination is witness discussion.

Study: Wright et al. (2000)

Wright et al. showed participants a picture story about a woman stealing a wallet. In one condition the woman was alone; in the other, she had an accomplice. Pairs of participants, one from each condition, then discussed the story. After the discussion each participant recalled individually. In 79% of cases, one member of each pair changed their recall (about the accomplice) following discussion.

Emotion/stress

Loftus and Burns (1982) found that participants who viewed a violent version of a video about a bank robbery were less able to recall the critical event. However, Yuille and Cutshall (1986) showed that recall of a real-life incident involving weapons was extremely accurate even months later.

Context

Godden and Baddeley (1975) showed how divers recalled more information if they learnt and recalled it in the same context (i.e. underwater). Malpass and Devine (1981) found that participants given contextual information showed better recall of an act of vandalism than those not given contextual information.

Expectations/stereotypes

Howitt (1991) found that recollections of a story were distorted by racist assumptions and Gruneberg (1992) found that witnesses to a staged mugging often believed that the (female) mugger was male.

Improving eyewitness recall: the cognitive interview

Fisher and Geiselman (1992) proposed the four-feature cognitive interview:
(1) The interviewer reinstates the context.
(2) Witnesses are asked to report every detail.
(3) Events are recalled in a different order.
(4) Events are recalled from different perspectives.

Study: Geiselman et al. (1985)

Geiselman et al. interviewed participants about a video of a crime using the cognitive interview and a standard interview. Witnesses recalled more items of information using the cognitive interview (41.2 correct items) than the standard interview (29.4 correct items).

Evaluation

- The cognitive interview improves recall except in young children (Geiselman, 1999).
- It is unclear whether all four features are essential (Milne and Bull, 2002).
- The enhancing effect decreases as time between event and interview increases.
- The cognitive interview enhances recall of events but not of people.

Knowledge check 21

Name two sources of post-event contamination.

Examiner tip
Questions about EW accounts are usually evidence-based so the discussion will tend to consist of evaluation of studies, use of evidence, comparison of relative importance of various factors and wider implications.

Knowledge check 22

What are the four features of the cognitive interview?

Children as eyewitnesses

Child witnesses can be less reliable than adults (Estgate and Groome, 2005). They are more affected by post-event contamination and their memories deteriorate more over time. They have difficulty distinguishing between memories for events they have experienced and memories from elsewhere (source monitoring).

Study: Poole and Lindsay (2001)

Poole and Lindsay tested children's ability to recall science demonstrations. They found that 35% of the children confused memory for actual demonstrations with memory for stories they had been told about other demonstrations. They concluded that young children find it difficult to monitor the source of a memory.

Evaluation

- Demand characteristics may be a factor. Ceci and Bruck (1993) suggested that children may give inaccurate details rather than not answer.
- Experiments involve recall of neutral rather than traumatic real-life events.
- Marin et al. (1979) found no difference in accuracy of identification and the effect of leading questions with age.

Flashbulb memory

Flashbulb memories are vivid memories of shocking events which include detail of the context. They are a special kind of source memory related to time and place of learning and may be linked to specific neural mechanisms. Some evidence indicates they are resistant to normal forgetting.

Study: Sharot et al. (2007)

Sharot et al. asked participants to recall the 9/11 attacks on the World Trade Center 3 years later. Those closest to the scene and therefore more personally shocked showed selective activation of the amygdala on MRI scans when recalling. Those who were further away did not show the same effect. Sharot concluded that highly arousing flashbulb memories involve a special neural mechanism.

Evaluation

- Flashbulb memories may appear stronger simply because of repeated retrieval.
- Neisser and Harsch (1992) found recall of the Challenger space shuttle disaster deteriorated over time.

The false memory debate

A recovered memory is where someone recalls an event of which they had no previous knowledge. A false memory is memory for an event that never happened. False memory syndrome (FMS) refers to a condition where someone has a memory of

source monitoring knowing whether a memory is of an event that you experienced or one that you have heard/read about from another source

Examiner tip

Be clear that you understand the debate: is it possible to have a memory of something that never happened (false), and/or is it possible to repress a memory of an event then later recall it (recovered)?

Knowledge check 23

What other possible explanations could there be for the failure of the women in the Williams study to recall their childhood abuse?

a traumatic experience (often childhood abuse) that never happened, but the person believes it did happen.

Controversy surrounding the recovery of repressed memories

Whether or not recovered memories can occur depends on Freud's theory of repression. Repression is a defence mechanism by which memories for unpleasant or upsetting events are 'pushed' into the unconscious. Some experimental evidence suggests repression is possible, for example Levinger and Clark (1961) found that participants were less likely to recall emotionally negative word associations than neutral ones.

Study: Williams (1994)

Williams interviewed women about their sexual histories. Although hospital records showed they had been abused as children, 38% of the women did not report the abusive event, suggesting they may have repressed the memories.

Study: Wright et al. (2006)

Wright et al. discussed recovered memory cases and argued that it is often uncertain (a) that the original event really happened, (b) that there was a time when the person could not consciously recall the event, and (c) whether eventual recall was actually spontaneous or a product of suggestion.

Evaluation

- Recovered memories may be a product of suggestion.
- Repression is unconscious so cannot be properly investigated.
- Memory in experiments is not like real-life memory for traumatic events.
- Williams' participants may have chosen not to discuss events they could remember.

The existence of false memories

False memories may be due to reconstruction. Loftus (2001) argued that people may begin to believe an event happened simply because a therapist uses guided imagination. Loftus and Ketcham (1994) showed memories can be implanted by suggestion.

Study: Loftus and Ketcham (1994)

Loftus and Ketcham introduced the idea of being 'lost in a shopping mall' in conversation. The topic was mentioned several times further and participants were asked about the event. Participants gradually became confident that they recalled the event, even giving detail they had not been told.

Study: Lindsay et al. (2004)

Lindsay et al. told students stories about events that had occurred while they were at school. Two events were real; one was fictitious. Around 25% recalled some detail of the fictitious event. With a photograph as a cue, around 33% recalled the fictitious event. This shows that people recall events that never happened, especially when given a cue.

Evaluation

- Events used in laboratory research are not like traumatic real-life memories.
- False memories may be affected by individual differences in suggestibility and meta-memory (awareness of own memory) (Wright et al., 2006).

Ethical and theoretical implications of the false memory debate

As most cases of false or recovered memory involve cases of childhood abuse, there are many ethical concerns: someone may be innocent and wrongly accused; family break-up and stigma; trauma for the patient, family and friends.

The theoretical implications relate to (a) Freud's psychoanalytic theory in general and the concept of repression, and (b) the theory of memory as active and reconstructive (Bartlett's schema theory and Loftus's work).

Examiner tip
These studies can also be used in questions about post-event contamination to explain how information given after the event affects recall.

Knowledge check 24
What is repression?

Summary

- Feature theory of face recognition suggests bottom-up, data-driven processing, based on features.
- Holistic theory suggests top-down, holistic processing with templates driving perception. Bruce and Young proposed a sequence: structural encoding > FRU > PIN > name generation.
- Composite systems: constructing a face from features. Initially paper-based, now computerised e.g. Evofit.
- Simultaneous line-ups: all members of the line-up appear together. Sequential line-ups: members of the line-up appear individually.
- Eyewitness accounts are often unreliable. Factors affecting reliability include post-event contamination, emotion, weapon focus, context and expectation. Post-event contamination can occur because of leading questions and witness discussion.
- The cognitive interview improves EW accuracy: reinstatement of context; reporting every detail;
events in different order; events from a different perspective.
- Child witnesses have difficulty with source monitoring.
- Flashbulb memories: vivid memories of a shocking event, tied to context, may involve special brain mechanisms.
- The false memory debate centres around recall of childhood events: (i) is the memory is false — never happened?; (ii) is the memory true — has been recovered after having been repressed?
- Loftus found false memories can be implanted through suggestion.
- Recovered memory is consistent with Freudian repression.
- There are ethical and theoretical implications of the debate.

Schizophrenia and mood disorders

Schizophrenia

Summary specification content

Classification of schizophrenia, including subtypes. Symptoms and diagnosis. Explanations, including biological and sociocultural — labelling and family dysfunction.

Treatments of schizophrenia, including anti-psychotic drugs and psychotherapy. The role of community care. Evaluation of these treatments.

Classification of schizophrenia

There are five sub-types:

- disorganised (hebephrenic) — disorganised speech, bizarre behaviour
- catatonic — excess motor activity or fixed, rigid posture (catatonic stupor)
- paranoid — delusions of grandeur/persecution, hallucinations
- residual — social withdrawal and flattened affect (emotion)
- undifferentiated — a mixture of symptoms from other sub-types

Evaluation

- The catatonic type is rare and may not be a separate category.
- The undifferentiated category is vague and over-used.
- It is difficult to distinguish between schizophrenia and similar disorders such as schizoaffective disorder.

Symptoms of schizophrenia

Positive symptoms:

- hallucinations — perceptions without external stimuli, e.g. hearing voices
- delusions — beliefs the sufferer thinks are true, of persecution or grandeur, e.g. 'I am Jesus'.
- thought and speech disturbances — unconnected, incoherent, 'word salad', thought insertion/broadcasting
- disorganised behaviour — unpredictable, excited or wild behaviour (catatonic excitement)

Negative symptoms:

- avolition (lack of will)
- flattened affect (no emotion)
- social isolation or withdrawal

Secondary symptoms

These are conditions that are a consequence of the disorder, such as depression, anxiety and alcohol abuse.

Examiner tip
Questions about the 'classification of schizophrenia' tend to be quite open. You may refer to the different subtypes, the symptoms and the difficulties/consequences of classification, both for the professional and for the patient.

AQA(B) A2 Psychology

Study: Kring and Neale (1996)

Kring and Neale observed schizophrenia sufferers and non-sufferers watching emotional films. Schizophrenia sufferers showed less facial expression during the film but reported similar levels of emotional experience afterwards. It seems that people with schizophrenia experience similar emotion but do not show it.

Diagnosis of schizophrenia

Two or more of the following core symptoms are required: delusions, hallucinations, disorganised speech, disorganised behaviour, negative symptoms. There should also be poor social/life functioning. Overall, there must be continuous disturbance for at least 6 months, with core symptoms for at least 1 month. Diagnosis is complicated because schizophrenia has three phases:

(1) prodomal — positive symptoms with normal life functioning
(2) active — strong positive symptoms
(3) residual — negative symptoms only

Diagnosis usually occurs in the active phase.

Evaluation

- Reliability is a problem.
- There may be ethnic bias.

Study: Goater et al. (1999)

Goater et al. monitored people from different ethnic groups for 5 years to see how many were diagnosed with schizophrenia. People from black ethnic minority groups were more likely to be diagnosed with schizophrenia.

Explanations of schizophrenia

The present view is that people may be biologically pre-disposed to the disorder, which can be triggered by stress (diathesis-stress model).

Biological explanations

Genetics

Schizophrenia may be inherited. Evidence comes from twin, family and adoption studies. Gottesman's (2001) review of more than 40 studies found concordance rates (both individuals in a pair have the disorder) increase as genetic similarity increases: identical (MZ) twins 48%, non-identical (DZ) twins 17% and siblings 9%. A child with one schizophrenic parent has a 1 in 8 chance of developing schizophrenia (Gottesman and Erlenmeyer-Kimling, 2001).

Knowledge check 25

What are the five subtypes of schizophrenia? Give a key symptom associated with each subtype.

diathesis-stress model a biological predisposition that is triggered by environmental stress

Study: Tienari (1991)

Tienari looked at the rates of schizophrenia in adopted children of mothers diagnosed with schizophrenia and controls whose mothers did not have schizophrenia. Approximately 10% of those with mothers with schizophrenia had schizophrenia, in contrast to 1% of the control group.

Evaluation

- The MZ rate is not 100%, suggesting the environment is also a factor.
- Higher MZ than DZ rates would also be predicted by environmentalists, as MZ pairs have a more shared environment than DZ pairs.
- No single schizophrenia gene has been identified.
- Early twin evidence is unreliable. Diagnosis was less rigorous and supposedly separated pairs were not really separated.

Biochemistry

Schizophrenia may be due to excess dopamine, a neurotransmitter. This may cause positive symptoms. Support for the dopamine hypothesis:

- post-mortems of schizophrenia sufferers show high levels of dopamine (Iversen, 1979)
- amphetamines and cocaine affect dopamine function and cause positive symptoms
- antipsychotic drugs (e.g. chlorpromazine) reduce dopamine activity and reduce positive symptoms

Evaluation

- Excess dopamine may be a cause or a consequence of the disorder.
- Other neurotransmitters, such as serotonin, are also involved (Breier, 1995).
- Some brain areas (i.e. the hypothalamus and amygdala) show excess dopamine, whereas others show levels below normal (i.e. the prefrontal cortex).
- Excess dopamine does not explain negative symptoms.
- The biological explanation is consistent with cognitive theories that people with schizophrenia have faulty information processing.

Other biological explanations

Schizophrenia sufferers show brain anomalies. For example, Weyandt (2006) found enlarged ventricles and Barch (2005) found that the prefrontal cortex is smaller and less active. Exposure of the mother to the flu virus in the second trimester has also been linked to schizophrenia in the child (Cannon, 1991).

Sociocultural explanations

Labelling

Szasz (1962) argued that the label 'schizophrenic' becomes a self-fulfilling prophecy so the person begins to conform to the label, showing more symptoms of the disorder.

Study: Rosenhan (1973)

Rosenhan asked eight **confederates** to go to hospital complaining of symptoms of schizophrenia. They were diagnosed and admitted, after which time they behaved completely normally and asked to be released. Hospital staff did not realise they were imposters and interpreted normal behaviours as symptoms. Their average stay was 17 days. They were discharged as 'schizophrenia in remission'.

Family dysfunction

Families of schizophrenia patients show high levels of conflict, communication problems and are highly critical and controlling. Mothers tend to be harsh and critical (schizophrenogenic). Bateson et al. (1956) referred to people with schizophrenia as being in a double bind or 'no win' situation where the parent's verbal and non-verbal messages conflict, causing the child to withdraw. Relapse is more likely when a recovering patient returns to a family high in expressed emotion (EE). Butzlaff and Hooley (1998) found relapse rates of 70% in high EE families compared to 30% in low EE families.

Evaluation

- Labelling does not explain how the disorder arises in the first place.
- EE may be because of the child's disturbed behaviour rather than a cause.
- Family-based explanations lead to blame.
- The family may be one source of stress in the diathesis-stress model.

Treatments of schizophrenia

Individuals respond differently to different treatments, but the most effective approach is probably a combination of drugs, psychotherapy and community care.

Anti-psychotic drugs

Conventional anti-psychotics are also called neuroleptics. Chlorpromazine was first used in the 1950s. It acts by blocking dopamine receptor sites, reducing dopamine activity and treating positive symptoms.

Study: Cole et al. (1964)

Cole et al. compared drug treatment with a control group. The drug group took chlorpromazine for 6 weeks while the control took a **placebo**. The drug group showed significant improvement (75%) compared to the placebo group (25%).

Atypical anti-psychotics (e.g. clozapine, risperidone) are new-generation drugs that reduce both positive and negative symptoms. They affect levels of dopamine and serotonin and are effective with patients who do not improve with conventional anti-psychotics.

confederate a person acting on behalf of the researcher, playing a role as part of the research

Examiner tip
The Rosenhan study can be used to answer various questions: to discuss the effects of labelling; to discuss the unreliability of diagnosis/classification; to discuss the effects of hospitalisation/institutionalisation versus community care.

Knowledge check 27
In what three ways might family dysfunction be involved in schizophrenia?

placebo a 'dummy' treatment with no active ingredient

Examiner tip

Explaining technical terms is helpful. For example, the revolving door syndrome: patients improve due to the medication then think they no longer need the medication, so stop taking it. This leads to relapse and the need for hospitalisation and so the cycle is repeated.

Evaluation

- Anti-psychotic drugs reduce the symptoms of schizophrenia.
- The drugs dramatically improve life for sufferers and families.
- One-quarter of patients do not respond to conventional anti-psychotics.
- The drugs must be taken continuously otherwise the symptoms return ('revolving door' syndrome).
- Side effects of conventional anti-psychotics include muscle tremors and tardive dyskinesia (jerky movements of the face and tongue).
- Side effects of new-generation drugs include nausea, weight gain, irregular heartbeat and (occasionally) an autoimmune disorder.

Psychotherapy

Any psychological (non-biological) therapy can be used here. Psychoanalytic therapy is of little use for people with schizophrenia, as patients have no insight. Cognitive therapy (Beck and Rector, 2006) attempts to help change negative attitudes and works on symptoms such as hearing voices. The therapist tries to change the patient's perception from feeling out of control (hearing things) to being in control, regarding the voices as someone trying to talk to them. Family therapy aims to increase tolerance, decrease criticism, reduce guilt and improve communication. Behavioural treatments based on operant conditioning or social learning theory have some effect on reducing bizarre behaviours. Token economies have been used in hospitals.

Study: Hogarty et al. (1986)

Examiner tip

The Hogarty study is a useful one. There are several treatment groups, it shows the importance of combining different treatments and there is a long-term follow-up one year later.

Hogarty et al. compared family therapy with other treatments. Patients received medication only, medication plus social skills training, medication plus family therapy or medication plus social skills training and family therapy. After 1 year, relapse rates were 40% for medication only, 20% for medication plus social skills training or family therapy, 0% for medication plus social skills training and family therapy combined.

Study: Paul and Lentz (1977)

Paul and Lentz studied a token economy in a hospital. Schizophrenia patients were given tokens for appropriate behaviours. The tokens could be exchanged for meals, cigarettes etc. Over 6 years, positive and negative symptoms reduced. However, when behaviour was no longer reinforced, some patients relapsed.

Evaluation

- Psychotherapies address different aspects of the disorder.
- Combined with medication, family therapy seems to work well.
- Token economies modify behaviour but do not treat the underlying disturbances.
- Token systems are ethically questionable as basic rights are withdrawn at the start.

The role of community care

Community care is an alternative to institutional care involving support in the community so sufferers can live as normal a life as possible. It may involve sheltered or supported living arrangements, ongoing therapy and enhancement of social skills.

Study: Stein and Test (1980)

Stein and Test compared the effectiveness of community care for schizophrenia patients over 12 months. One group received hospital treatment with medication and was then discharged without support. The community care group had training in skills and educational support after discharge. Most of the unsupported patients had to be re-admitted to hospital within the year, whereas most of the community care group remained living in the community.

Evaluation

- Adequately supported community care is preferable to the stigma and negative effects of institutionalisation.
- If support is withdrawn, relapse is likely.
- Medication needs to be careful monitored.

Mood disorders

Summary specification content

Unipolar and bipolar depression. Symptoms and diagnosis of unipolar and bipolar depression. Explanations, including biological, cognitive and psychodynamic.

Treatments of mood disorders, including biological and cognitive.

Evaluation of these treatments.

Unipolar and bipolar depression

With unipolar depression, the patient's mood is at the low end of the mood spectrum. Symptoms include:

- emotional (e.g. sadness, loss of pleasure and guilt)
- cognitive (e.g. poor concentration and memory)
- physiological (e.g. sleep disturbances, headaches and tiredness)
- behavioural (e.g. social withdrawal and poor hygiene)

Clinical diagnosis of depression requires at least five symptoms for at least 2 weeks. Onset may be gradual or sudden. People who have had one major depressive episode are at risk of further episodes. Depression is twice as likely in women as men (Nolen-Hoeksema, 2002) across all age groups and cultures.

With bipolar depression, the patient suffers extreme mood swings between deep depression and mania. Mania symptoms include euphoria, highly elevated mood, grand plans, irrational decisions, high energy, rapid speech and little sleep. In the manic phase the person may stop taking medication. After the manic phase there may be deep depression and exhaustion.

> **Examiner tip**
>
> Community care is not a treatment but should be seen as a care option, the alternative to which is hospitalisation. Consider the strengths/limitations of community care, and compare it with hospital care. It is a mistake to assume that patients in hospital are treated solely with drugs, whereas patients in the community receive solely psychological therapies.

> **Knowledge check 28**
>
> Give two strengths and two limitations of community care for patients with schizophrenia.

Diagnosis of bipolar disorder requires both a major depressive episode and a manic episode. Some 1–2% of adults suffer from bipolar depression, with equal rates for men and women (Shastry, 2005). Onset is usually around 20 years.

Explanations of mood disorders

The biological and cognitive explanations are the strongest for unipolar depression and the biological is the preferred explanation for bipolar depression.

Biological explanations

Genetics

Family/twin studies suggest a genetic basis, with a family history increasing the risk of developing the disorder. Twin studies show higher concordance rates for identical (MZ) twins. The genetic contribution in bipolar depression seems to be much higher than in unipolar depression. Research indicates an abnormal serotonin transporter (SERT) gene could play a key role (Southwick, 2005)

Study: McGuffin (1996)

McGuffin studied 177 sets of twins. For unipolar depression, the concordance rates were 46% for identical (MZ) twins and 20% for non-identical (DZ) twins, indicating a genetic component.

Study: Price (1968)

In a study of bipolar disorder, Price found concordance of 68% for MZs raised together, 67% for separated MZs and 23% for DZs. These rates indicate a genetic component for bipolar depression.

Biochemistry

The neurotransmitters serotonin and norepinephrine are involved in unipolar and bipolar disorders. Both affect energy levels, sleep, hunger and activity, and are found in the limbic system which controls sleep, appetite and emotions. Low levels cause depression, although it is now thought to be due to an interaction between the two (Thase, 2002). Depression has also been linked to high levels of cortisol, which is released by the endocrine system at times of stress. In depressed people the high cortisol level seems to be maintained even after the stressful event has disappeared (Southwick et al., 2005).

In bipolar disorder, serotonin is low in the manic phase and norepinephrine is high (Shastry, 2005). In the depression phase, both are low. Bipolar depression has also been linked to abnormal ion activity at the neuronal membrane, resulting in abnormal electrical impulses in the neuron.

Brain abnormalities

Brain scans suggest abnormality in four areas of the brain may be associated with depression: prefrontal cortex, hippocampus, anterior cingulated cortex and amygdala.

Examiner tip
Look critically at the concordance rates for the Price study. The concordance rates for MZs reared together and MZs reared apart are almost identical, indicating a strong genetic component because the different environments appear to have had scarcely any effect.

Evaluation

- No single gene for mood disorders has been identified.
- Reserpine (a medication for high blood pressure) reduces levels of serotonin and epinephrine and can cause depression.
- Some research into postnatal depression suggests it is due to social factors rather than hormone changes (Hendrick et al., 1998).
- Brain abnormalities and high or low levels of brain chemicals may be a consequence of depression rather than a cause.
- Twin studies have the same problems as for schizophrenia.

Cognitive explanations

Cognitive psychologists suggest depression is due to negative thinking (Beck, 1987). Negative schemas develop in childhood and adolescence. Negative thinking involves:

- over-generalisation (one bad thing means everything is bad)
- magnification/catastrophisation (blowing up events out of proportion)
- selective perception of negative events
- absolutism (if things are not perfect, it is a disaster)

Beck proposed the cognitive triad, stating that depressed people think negatively about themselves, the world and the future.

schema unit of knowledge

Study: Alloy et al. (1999)

Alloy et al. identified students as either 'optimistic' thinkers or 'hopeless' thinkers. The students were interviewed regularly over 2½ years. Only 1% of those with an optimistic thinking style developed depression, compared to 17% of those with a hopeless thinking style.

Study: Beck (1976)

Beck gave the dysfunctional attitude scale (DAS) to depressed and non-depressed people. Those with depression scored higher on the DAS, showing they thought more negatively about events and situations than non-depressed people.

According to the attribution-helplessness model of depression (Peterson and Seligman, 1984; Abramson et al., 2002), depressed people make internal, stable, global attributions for negative events, i.e. they blame themselves.

Examiner tip
The Alloy findings support the cognitive explanation. Although we cannot assume cause and effect, it suggests that negative thinkers are more likely to develop depression.

Evaluation

- Cognitive explanations are based on research with people.
- Cognitive factors cannot explain the manic phase in bipolar depression.
- Cognitive explanations have led to effective cognitive therapies.

Psychodynamic explanations

Freud (1917) explained depression in terms of grief (loss) and dependency. Grief as a result of early loss turns to anger, which is turned inward and results in self-blame (introjection of hostility). Loss in adulthood brings back feelings of loss experienced as a child, causing depression.

Another psychodynamic explanation is that depression results from failure to meet the excessively high demands of over-harsh parents. In adulthood this leads to depression due to unattainable standards and ideals. Klein et al. (2002) found depression is associated with dependency, perfectionism and low self-esteem.

According to Freud, bipolar depression is due to interaction between the id, ego and superego. When the superego dominates, this causes guilt, leading to depression. The ego tries to control the superego and over-reaction leads to the manic phase.

Evaluation

- There is little scientific evidence, although Bowlby's work on attachment and loss was based on research.
- Psychodynamic explanations have given way to interpersonal theories, such as contingency self-worth theory (Kuiper and Olinger, 1986).

Treatments of mood disorders

For unipolar depression, a combination of drugs and cognitive therapy seems most effective. For bipolar depression, drug therapy is preferred.

Biological treatments

Drug therapy

Antidepressant drugs affect neurotransmitter levels. They include:
- tricyclics, which act to increase the activity of norepinephrine and serotonin
- MAOIs (monoamine oxidase inhibitors), which stop the breakdown of norepinephrine
- SSRIs (selective serotonin reuptake inhibitors) such as Prozac (fluoxetine), which prolong serotonin activity at the synapse

Evaluation

- Effectiveness rates: tricylics 60%, MAOIs 50% and SSRIs about 60% (Comer, 2008). SSRIs are fast-acting (around 2 weeks).
- Tricyclic side effects include dry mouth, perspiration, constipation and sexual dysfunction.
- MAOIs have serious side effects without a strict diet.
- Side effects of SSRIs include anxiety, agitation and reported increased risk of suicide.
- Not everyone responds to medication and it does not work immediately.

For bipolar disorder, lithium is used. It alters activity in the neuron and in doing so may restore levels of neurotransmitters to normal. It is most effective for mania. Dosage must be carefully monitored and there are unpleasant side effects (possible

introjection turning emotions inwards towards the self

Examiner tip

A considered discussion of mood disorders should recognise that the disorder probably has multiple causes. For example, an innate predisposition (biological) may be triggered by childhood events (psychodynamic) and result in faulty thinking (cognitive).

kidney dysfunction). Patients often stop taking lithium during the manic phase, leading to relapse.

Electroconvulsive therapy (ECT)

ECT induces a brain seizure by passing electricity through the brain. Anaesthetic and muscle relaxant are given, then electrodes are placed on the head (bilateral or unilateral) and an electric shock is given. The seizure usually lasts around a minute. A course of 6–12 sessions is typical. It is used with cases that do not respond to medication and is effective for 50% of people (Fink, 2001).

Evaluation

- The mode of action is not known.
- Side effects include memory loss, guilt and possible permanent damage.
- Relapse rates are high (80%) and further treatment is often required.

Cognitive treatments

Rational emotive therapy (RET) Ellis (1984)

RET attempts to replace irrational thoughts with rational ones. The therapist challenges irrational beliefs through confrontation and argument.

Cognitive behaviour therapy (CBT) Beck (1993)

CBT focuses on changing the cognitive triad in four phases:
(1) increasing confidence and elevating mood
(2) challenging automatic negative thoughts
(3) identifying biased thinking
(4) changing attitudes and beliefs

Beck's therapy involves 'the patient as scientist'. The patient sets hypotheses to test negative beliefs and gathers evidence to challenge them. Between sessions a diary is used to monitor thoughts.

Study: Hollon et al. (2006)

Hollon et al. compared the effectiveness of cognitive therapy and drug therapy for depression. Over 16 weeks, patients received drug therapy or cognitive therapy. After 1 year, approximately 40% of the cognitive therapy group had relapsed, compared to 45% of the drug therapy group. A placebo group showed around 80% relapse.

Evaluation

- Cognitive therapy is effective, especially when combined with drug therapy.
- Cognitive therapy is not helpful in the manic phase of bipolar depression.
- Patients need to be reasonably articulate and well motivated.

Knowledge check 29

Name four classes of drugs used to treat mood disorders. Which one of these is used solely for bipolar disorder?

Examiner tip

It is an overstatement to suggest that ECT is 'barbaric' and 'hardly ever used' these days. In fact, it is still used with cases that do not respond to medication and is sometimes highly effective.

Knowledge check 30

Suggest three ways a cognitive behaviour therapist might treat a depressed person who thinks she is worthless because she has lost her job.

Summary

Schizophrenia

- The five subtypes: disorganised, catatonic, paranoid, residual, undifferentiated.
- Symptoms include: hallucinations, delusions, thought/speech disturbances, disorganised behaviour, flattened affect, avolition.
- Biological explanations focus on genetics, excess dopamine (activity), brain anomalies, prenatal flu virus exposure.
- Sociocultural explanations include labelling and family dysfunction.
- Antipsychotic drugs include chlorpromazine (blocks dopamine activity) and atypical anti-psychotics e.g. clozapine.
- Psychotherapies include cognitive, family and behavioural therapy.
- Community care is an alternative to hospitalisation.

Mood disorders

- Unipolar — low mood. Bipolar — mood varies from low to high.
- Symptoms are emotional, cognitive, physiological and behavioural.
- Biological explanations include: genetics; biochemistry — low serotonin (and norepinephrine); brain abnormalities; bipolar — abnormal ion activity.
- Cognitive explanations include: negative schemas; the cognitive triad; attribution-helplessness.
- Psychodynamic explanations focus on grief/loss, dependency, introjection of hostility.
- Biological treatments include SSRIs, MAOIs, tricyclics (lithium for bipolar disorder).
- ECT is a biological treatment.
- Cognitive therapy: challenging and replacing negative beliefs; patient 'as scientist'.

Stress and stress management

Stress and illness

Summary specification content

The role of the automatic nervous system (ANS) and endocrine system functions in mediating and responding to stress.

Ways of measuring stress, including physiological, behavioural and self-report techniques.

The role of personal variables, including behaviour types A, B and C, locus of control and hardiness in mediating responses to stress.

Stress has been linked to illness (Kimvaki et al., 2002). People under stress also behave unhealthily, for example they have a poor diet and drink more alcohol, which may increase risk of illness (Ng and Jeffery, 2003). Johnson (2002) distinguished between chronic stress (over a sustained period) and acute stress (over a short period). Chronic stress affects the autonomic nervous system.

Study: Cohen et al. (1991)

Cohen et al. exposed participants to the cold virus. They also completed a stress questionnaire and were classified as high or low stress. In the high stress group, 47% developed a cold compared to only 27% in the low stress group.

Examiner tip
Note that the title for this subsection is 'stress and illness' so be ready to explain the relationship between the two.

The role of the autonomic nervous system (ANS)

The ANS is responsible for autonomic (involuntary) functions. It is comprised of sympathetic and parasympathetic sections. The sympathetic section prepares the body for action (flight or fight) by increasing heart rate. The parasympathetic section restores body functioning to normal.

Examiner tip

Refer back at this point to what you learned about the autonomic nervous system for Unit 1.

The role of the endocrine system

The endocrine system is made up of glands that secrete hormones into the bloodstream. The pituitary gland and adrenal gland are involved in the body's response to stress.

When a stressor is perceived, the sympathetic section of the ANS is activated: the adrenal medulla releases adrenaline and noradrenaline, increasing heart rate and blood flow. Meanwhile the hypothalamus produces corticotropin-releasing factor (CRF), stimulating the pituitary gland to secrete adrenocorticotrophic hormone (ACTH). This enters the circulation and stimulates the adrenal cortex to produce corticosteroids (including the hormone cortisol), which control glucose metabolism. These fight inflammation but can weaken the immune system causing illness over a sustained stressful period (Vedhara et al., 1999).

Long-term exposure to stress and continued bodily arousal is damaging; prolonged cardiovascular reactivity can cause strokes (Dougall and Baum, 2001). Schnall et al. (1990) found enlarged hearts in people with stressful jobs and Patterson et al. (1995) found increased blood cholesterol.

Knowledge check 31

Explain the role of the adrenal medulla and the hypothalamus in responding to stress.

Study: Willis et al. (1987)

Willis et al. studied cortisol levels over time. Participants contacted the researchers when they experienced a stressful incident. Levels were measured at the time and afterwards. Cortisol was raised at the time of the incident and lower afterwards.

cortisol a hormone that fights inflammation but can weaken the immune system over time

Evaluation

- Explaining stress purely in physiological terms is reductionist. Experience and feelings are also important.
- Some moderate or brief stress can be beneficial (eustress), stimulating the cardiovascular and respiratory systems.

Ways of measuring stress

Physiological techniques

Hormone levels (corticosteroids and catecholamines) can be determined using blood and urine samples. Blood pressure, heart rate, rate of breathing and galvanic skin responses (GSR) can be measured.

Polygraphs allow for a number of physiological measures at the same time. A baseline is established before there is exposure to a stressor. Physiological changes are recorded.

GSR or galvanic skin response minute changes in conductivity in the skin's surface moisture that occur with arousal, and which can be measured from recordings from tiny electrodes

Evaluation

- Physiological measures are objective.
- Arousal is not the same as stress. Other factors create arousal, e.g. humour.
- Special equipment and training are required.
- The measures themselves may be stressful.
- Variables such as weight and exercise can affect the results.

Behavioural techniques

Everyday behaviours can be measured (e.g. rate of speech) or more controlled measures may be taken in a laboratory. Typical laboratory stressors are loud noise, overcrowding, electric shocks and extreme temperature. Behavioural stress measures include aggression (verbal or non-verbal) and speech measures such as stuttering.

Study: Glass and Singer (1972)

Glass and Singer exposed participants to loud noise while a control group worked in the quiet. The control group performed better on problem-solving and proofreading tasks. The researchers concluded that noise stressors have a negative effect on cognitive tasks.

Evaluation

- Performance measures are objective.
- Exposure to unpleasant stressors may be unethical.
- Laboratory stress is artificial.
- Behavioural techniques measure the consequences of stress rather than a person's experience of stress.

Self-report techniques

Self-report measures involve people reporting their stress-related behaviours or assessing their experience of stress/stress events. Rating scales and questionnaires are used, although some studies use interviews or diaries.

The Holmes and Rahe (1967) Social Readjustment Rating Scale (SRRS) is a questionnaire about stressful life events occurring in the previous year. Each event has a score. A high score on the SRRS means a person is highly stressed and vulnerable to stress-related illness.

Evaluation

- The SRRS is crude and neglects individual differences.
- Giving a single score is an oversimplification.
- A stressful event can be negative for one person and positive for another (e.g. divorce).
- Many SRRS events occur rarely. A better measure may be the Hassles and Uplifts Scale (Kanner et al., 1981), which focuses on small everyday hassles.

Examiner tip
Check out examples of the SRRS online for examples of life events from the scale to illustrate your evaluation points.

Peacock and Wong's (1990) Stress Appraisal Measure (SAM) is another self-report measure. It measures stress (real or potential) by scoring events for potential harm (threat), challenge and perceived importance.

Evaluation
- Questionnaires and ratings are quick and easy to administer.
- Self-report measures require insight, which people do not always have.
- The measures are subjective.

Knowledge check 32

Identify three ways of measuring stress.

The role of personal variables in mediating responses to stress

Type A, B and C behaviours

Friedman and Rosenman (1974) identified a personality type that is more likely to respond negatively to stress: the type A personality. Friedman and Rosenman (1959) suggested type A people were more at risk of heart disease than type Bs. More recent research has focused on one aspect of type A (anger and hostility) in coronary heart disease (Kop and Krantz, 1997).

Type A people show competitiveness and achievement orientation, time urgency, anger and hostility.

Type B people are easy going, uncompetitive, friendly and positive and show low time urgency.

Study: Friedman and Rosenman (1959)

Friedman and Rosenman interviewed men about work, exercise, diet etc. Their cholesterol levels and heart function were also measured. Using colleague assessments, the men were identified as type A or type B. Type A men were more likely than type Bs to be at risk of heart disease. They worked longer hours and had a family history of heart disease.

Type C has recently been linked to susceptibility to cancer. Type C people are passive, uncomplaining and compliant. Holland and Lewis (1996) argue that emotional suppression may lead to illness. Cohen and Herbert (1996) have linked type C with depression.

Examiner tip

Focus on both Type A and Type C as affecting stress.

Evaluation
- Assessment usually involves interviews and behavioural observation so the outcome has some reliability.
- Hostility may be more important than other elements of type A.
- Myrtek (2001) argued that type A could not usefully predict heart disease.
- Type B and type C show some overlap.

Locus of control

Locus of control is a person's perceived control over what happens to them (Rotter, 1966). People with an internal locus of control believe they are in control of events in their life. High (not extreme) internal control is associated with less physical and psychological illness. Those with external locus believe they are not in control of what happens to them and extreme external locus can lead to helplessness, stress and depression. An extreme internal locus can also cause stress because it is impossible to control all events in our life. A balanced locus of control leads to low stress.

Study: Frankenhauser (1975)

Frankenhauser studied workers in a monotonous and dull job at a saw mill, measuring catecholamine levels, blood pressure, reported headaches and stomach problems. The workers showed high stress levels on all measures due to their lack of control over their boring work.

Evaluation

- Locus of control is assessed by the self-report locus of control scale and is therefore subjective.
- People may have perceived control in some areas of life and not others.

Hardiness

Kobasa (1979) identified hardiness as three traits that together appear to help resist the effects of stress:
- commitment (to family, job, community etc.)
- seeing events as a challenge or opportunity rather than an threat
- control (autonomy over own life)

Hardy people have a sense of purpose. They feel in control and thrive on challenge, perceiving stressful events positively.

Study: Kobasa et al. (1982)

Kobasa et al. assessed a large sample of US executives for hardiness. They were also measured for stressful life experiences and illness. Those with high hardiness scores had less illness than those with low hardiness scores, even though their level of exposure to stress was the same.

Evaluation

- Even hardy people are eventually worn down by stress (burn out) (Rowe, 1997).
- Most research uses self-reporting and is therefore subjective.
- Hardiness may apply to men rather than women.

Stress management

Summary specification content

Problem-focused and emotion-focused strategies. The role of defence mechanisms in coping with stress, including repression, regression, rationalisation and denial.

Techniques of stress management: behavioural approaches, including biofeedback and systematic desensitisation; cognitive therapy.

The role of social factors in coping with stress: social support, including types of social support.

Lazarus (1993) proposed a two-stage model of stress appraisal. The transactional model explains how stress results from interaction between the event and how the person appraises the event. In primary appraisal, the person considers whether the event is potentially stressful. In secondary appraisal, the person decides whether he or she has the ability to cope (self-efficacy).

Examiner tip

Discussion of the difference between primary and secondary appraisal could be useful for analysis.

Problem-focused and emotion-focused strategies

Lazarus (1999) suggested strategies can be:
- problem-focused — addressing the problem or event causing the stress
- emotion-focused — addressing the emotional reaction to stress

Folkman (1986) identified eight coping strategies.

Problem-focused strategies include:
- planful problem-solving — developing and executing a plan to deal with the stressor
- confronting — tackling the problem 'head on', which need not be aggressive

Emotion-focused strategies include:
- distancing — putting the problem at a distance, e.g. through humour
- positive reappraisal — seeing the positive side of the situation, 'looking on the bright side'

Knowledge check 34

Give a concrete example of how a person might use (i) a problem-focused strategy and (ii) an emotion-focused strategy to cope with losing a job.

Study: Billings and Moos (1981)

Billings and Moos asked married couples about how they coped with a recent crisis. Males and females tended to use more problem-focused than emotion-focused strategies. However, women used more emotion-focused strategies than men. All preferred emotion-focused strategies for personal loss (e.g. death).

Evaluation
- Different stressors require different strategies.
- Strategies are often used in combination.
- Research focuses on identification of strategies rather than effectiveness.
- Individuals differ in their ability to use strategies. Nolen-Hoeksema et al. (1997) point out that 'ruminators' who dwell on problems are less likely to address the issue.

Examiner tip

Be clear that defence mechanisms operate at an unconscious level. This means that we do not consciously 'use' them

The role of defence mechanisms

According to the psychodynamic approach, unconscious defence mechanisms help us to cope with unpleasant stressful events and thoughts. They are emotion-focused strategies in that they do not address the problem directly. Instead, they reduce the emotional response.

- Repression involves unconsciously pushing memories of an unpleasant stressful event from conscious awareness. Freud believed that repressed memories may manifest themselves as anxiety disorders at some later time.
- Regression involves reverting to childlike behaviour to relieve the experience of stress.
- Rationalisation involves explaining an unpleasant stressful event in positive terms.
- Denial involves refusing to acknowledge that an unpleasant stressful event is happening. Denial helps in the short term, giving time to adjust, but the problem may persist or worsen.

Evaluation

- Most defence mechanisms help in the short term only.
- In the long term, they may be damaging.
- Some defence mechanisms, such as intellectualisation, can be productive in the long term.
- Defence mechanisms are unconscious so cannot be studied.

Knowledge check 35

Explain why defence mechanisms as a way of coping with stress might be damaging in the long term.

Techniques of stress management

Behavioural approaches

Behavioural approaches aim to change behaviour to help reduce stress.

Biofeedback

Biofeedback is based on operant conditioning principles. Physiological functions (e.g. heart rate) are monitored and feedback (visual or auditory) is given. As the physiological functions fluctuate (e.g. heart rate slows minutely), **positive reinforcement** is given. This may simply be seeing the lower readout on the monitor. The person can then work to try to reduce the heart rate further and receive more reinforcement. Training is laboratory-based. Thermal biofeedback is sometimes used for stress because skin temperature is low when stressed.

positive reinforcement a pleasant stimulus as a consequence of a desired behaviour — makes the behaviour more likely to be repeated

Study: Scharff et al. (2002)

Scharff et al. trained children who suffered stress migraines in hand-warming biofeedback. There were two other groups: a hand-cooling group and a control group. The hand-warming group reported fewer migraines than other groups for up to 6 months.

Evaluation
- Biofeedback is effective for anxiety and headaches (Gatchel et al., 1989).
- Biofeedback may be no better than simple relaxation (Lehrer et al., 1994).
- There may be a placebo effect.
- The technique is difficult to use in real-life situations.

Examiner tip
Explain evaluation points in full. For example, why is biofeedback difficult to use in real-life situations?

Systematic desensitisation
Systematic desensitisation involves the gradual systematic exposure to a stressor. Graded exposure to a stimulus hierarchy is combined with relaxation techniques to help the person deal with the stressful stimulus. The technique is based on classical conditioning principles, counter-conditioning the person to feel calm.

Study: Morrow et al. (1992)
Morrow et al. studied systematic desensitisation with cancer patients receiving chemotherapy. The systematic desensitisation group was compared with a control group for duration of nausea after chemotherapy. On average the control group experienced 15 hours, more nausea than the treatment group. The treatment reduced the stress of chemotherapy and the side effects.

Evaluation
- It cannot help where stress is unexpected.
- It treats the response to stress rather than the cause.

Knowledge check 36
Name two behavioural techniques used to manage stress.

Cognitive therapy
Cognitive therapy involves cognitive restructuring to replace negative thoughts caused by stress.

Rational emotive therapy (RET)
This was proposed by Ellis (1962). Ellis said that people often have irrational beliefs that lead them to feel stressed (e.g. 'I must be loved and accepted by everyone I meet'). As a result, they catastrophise and feel unable to cope. RET helps the person replace irrational and catastrophic beliefs with rational, positive and realistic beliefs. RET involves rational confrontation where the therapist challenges the client's irrational beliefs through robust argument.

Stress inoculation training (SIT)
Meichenbaum (1996) proposed three stages of SIT:
(1) conceptualisation (the stress is understood)
(2) skills acquisition (skills to manage the stress are rehearsed, e.g. positive self-talk)
(3) application (skills are applied)

SIT has been used with patients before surgery and to manage pain (Meichenbaum, 1996). Training is flexible, varying from a single, short session to hourly sessions over many weeks.

Study: Jaremko (2006)

Jaremko used SIT with students to control the stress of public speaking. Participants reported less anxiety (stress) after being trained in SIT.

Evaluation
- Cognitive and behavioural techniques can be successful in combination.
- Cognitive therapies recognise that stress often involves distorted thinking, which affects behaviour and emotion.
- Many people find RET too aggressive.
- RET techniques are most suitable for articulate and motivated clients.
- SIT is flexible and can be used with individuals, couples and small groups.

The role of social factors in coping with stress

Social support usually comes from friends, neighbours, family etc. It may buffer the effect of stress (Cohen and Wills, 1985). Cohen et al. (1986) found that social support is greater for people with good communication and social skills.

Stroebe (2000) noted five types of social support:
- appraisal support — others help the person understand the stressors
- emotional support — others show love/care
- esteem support — others help strengthen feelings of self-worth
- informational support — others give advice and guidance (this may be professional)
- instrumental support — others provide practical help

Study: Sosa et al. (1980)

Sosa et al. investigated the effects of instrumental support in childbirth. Women in one group received social support during labour. A control group had no extra social support. The social support group reported a better experience and had much shorter labours than the control group. Instrumental social support helped with the stress of labour.

Study: Berkman and Syme (1979)

Berkman and Syme followed a large sample over 9 years, recording social support using questionnaires on marital status, friends etc. They found that those with little social support were more likely to die during the study.

Evaluation
- Social support varies according to gender (women offer emotional support more than men) and culture (support from extended family is more common in traditional cultures).
- Too much social support can be overwhelming and add to stress.
- Social support is so varied it is difficult to assess the effectiveness.
- Social support is measured using self-report, which is subjective.

- The ANS and endocrine system mediate response to stress.
- The ANS comprises the sympathetic section and parasympathetic section.
- The endocrine system releases hormones: adrenal medulla releases adrenalin and noradrenalin; hypothalamus releases CRF; pituitary releases ACTH; adrenal cortex produces cortisol. Cortisol fights inflammation but can affect the immune system.
- Stress can be measured using physiological, behavioural and self-report techniques.
- Personal variables mediating response to stress include personality type, locus of control and hardiness.
- Ways of managing stress can be emotion focused or problem focused.
- Defence mechanisms are emotion focused e.g. repression, regression, rationalisation and denial.
- Behavioural approaches to stress management include biofeedback and systematic desensitisation.
- Cognitive therapies for stress include rational emotive therapy (RET) and stress inoculation training (SIT).
- Social support includes appraisal, emotional, esteem, informational and instrumental support.

Substance abuse

Use and abuse

Summary specification content

Physical and psychological dependence, tolerance and withdrawal in relation to nicotine, alcohol, stimulants and depressants.

Explanations for substance abuse: hereditary factors; personality characteristics and social factors, including peer influences.

Substance use is where taking a substance involves no harm. Substance abuse is where the substance harms either the person taking it or others. What is use and abuse varies in different societies.

Physical and psychological dependence

Addiction occurs when, with repeated use, someone becomes preoccupied with a substance and dependent on it. The addictive behaviour causes a pleasant feeling (high). In **physical dependence**, the body has got used to the substance and needs it to be in a 'normal' state, i.e. without withdrawal symptoms. This is because drugs act by changing brain chemistry.

In **psychological dependence**, there is an emotional and mental compulsion to keep taking the substance — a belief that the substance is necessary. The drug becomes the focus of life and determines daily routines. There is craving — a motivational state of want and desire — for the drug.

Tolerance

Tolerance occurs when the body adapts to the substance over time and so more is required to have the same physical and psychological effects. Some drugs, such as cannabis, do not result in tolerance.

physical dependence the body needs the substance to function normally

psychological dependence belief that the substance is necessary

Examiner tip

The Siegel study is useful to illustrate the complexity of tolerance and how tolerance is not simply physiological but can also be influenced by the context in which the drug is taken. It is not really very useful in an answer on explanations for substance abuse.

Siegel et al.'s (1982) theory of conditioned drug tolerance explains how the same level of drug usage, but in different settings, can result in drug overdose.

Study: Siegel et al. (1982)

Siegel et al. gave rats heroin in their usual environment for 80 days. Half the rats were then put in a different environment and the other half remained in the usual place. All rats were then given a high dose of heroin. Many of those in the new environment died of the overdose (65%), compared with only 30% in the usual environment.

Withdrawal

Withdrawal is the unpleasant physical and psychological side effects experienced when use of a drug is suddenly stopped. Withdrawal occurs if a drug has been used for some time and tolerance has developed. The effects are usually the opposite of the pleasant effects of a drug. Symptoms are unpleasant so relapse is likely. Withdrawal requires careful management.

- Nicotine withdrawal symptoms include cravings, depression, sleep problems.
- Alcohol withdrawal symptoms include sweating, anxiety, nausea, tremors and cramps.
- Heroin withdrawal symptoms include anxiety, pain, diarrhoea, shivering and sweating.

Knowledge check 37

Explain what is meant by tolerance and withdrawal.

Nicotine

Tobacco contains nicotine, a mild stimulant. Nicotine enters the bloodstream rapidly and levels decline rapidly. This means that someone must smoke regularly to keep the nicotine at a certain level. Factors that explain why people start to smoke include peer pressure, role models, parents and friends smoking, rebelliousness and risk-taking personality.

Robinson and Klesges (1997) found teenagers think smoking projects a grown-up image. One biological explanation is the nicotine regulation model.

nicotine regulation model a biological theory of nicotine addiction that states that there is a physiological drive to maintain the level of nicotine in the body to avoid withdrawal symptoms

Study: Schachter et al. (1977)

Schachter et al. asked smokers to smoke low-nicotine cigarettes for one week and high-nicotine cigarettes for the next week. Participants smoked more low-nicotine than high-nicotine cigarettes. It seems that smokers try to maintain a certain nicotine level in the body, supporting the biological nicotine regulation model.

Korsakoff's syndrome a progressive, degenerative disease caused by excessive and prolonged alcohol consumption; it affects the function of the nervous system, eventually leading to dementia and death

Alcohol

Alcohol is absorbed quickly into the bloodstream. It is addictive and leads to tolerance if it is drunk every day. It causes physical and psychological dependence. Negative effects of heavy drinking on health include liver disease and amnesia (Korsakoff's syndrome). Alcohol use has been linked to aggression and antisocial personality (Zucker et al., 1996).

Stimulants

These stimulate the central nervous system, causing euphoria and energy. They include amphetamines (e.g. ecstasy), cocaine and alkyl nitrites ('poppers'). Amphetamines increase heart rate and blood supply to the muscles and increase dopamine levels in the brain. Tolerance develops quickly. Withdrawal symptoms include exhaustion and depression. Ecstasy is a hallucinogenic amphetamine. Animal studies show it can damage nerve cells. Cocaine has immediate but short-lived effects of wellbeing and confidence. Tolerance does not develop and withdrawal effects are not severe in comparison to alcohol and heroin. Alkyl nitrites dilate the blood vessels and are meant to enhance sexual performance. After-effects include headaches and nausea.

Depressants

Depressants induce calmness by slowing down central nervous system activity. High doses of depressants can cause unconsciousness. Alcohol and solvents are depressants. Others include opiates (e.g. heroin), tranquillisers (e.g. diazepam) and barbiturates (sleeping pills). Heroin (a Class A drug) can be injected or smoked and is thought to be highly addictive. It results in euphoria but a tolerance soon develops. Tranquillisers (Class B drugs) are prescribed for anxiety disorders. They act to release GABA, a neurotransmitter, which results in calmness and sleep. They are usually prescribed for short-term use as tolerance and dependence develop easily. Withdrawal symptoms include insomnia, sweating, tremors, loss of appetite and irritability.

Explanations for substance abuse

Hereditary factors

A predisposition to alcohol abuse may be genetic. Melo et al. (1996) selectively bred animals that preferred alcohol with one another. The offspring were found to prefer alcohol to other drinks. Human twin research suggests there may be a predisposition to substance abuse and dependence.

Study: Kaij (1960)

Kaij studied alcohol abuse in identical (MZ) twins and non-identical (DZ) twins. The concordance rate was 54% in MZ pairs and 28% in DZ pairs. This result supports the genetic explanation for alcohol abuse.

Evaluation

- Even MZ pairs are not 100% concordant.
- Higher MZ than DZ rates would also be predicted by environmentalists as MZ pairs have a more shared environment than DZ pairs.
- Twin studies often use small samples and can be unreliable (in early studies MZ or DZ status was not always clear).

Adoption studies compare adopted children with their biological parents. Adoptees who abused alcohol as adults were likely to have a biological parent who abused alcohol (Goldstein, 1994). Peters and Preedy (2002) reported that 18% of adoptees

Examiner tip

Remember that alcohol is a depressant, so you could use what you know about alcohol abuse in a question about depressants.

Knowledge check 38

Identify two stimulants and two depressants.

Examiner tip

If you use the Melo study in your answer you need to explain the process of selective breeding and how the study supports the genetic view.

with a biological parent who abused alcohol became alcohol abusers compared to 5% of adoptees in a control group. One large-scale adoption study by Cloninger (1987) showed that approximately 17% of sons of alcohol-abusing fathers became alcohol abusers, as opposed to approximately 3% of controls.

Gene mapping techniques have found abnormal dopamine-linked genes in 60% of alcohol abusers and 50% of people who use cocaine regularly (Melo et al., 1996).

Evaluation

- Biological explanations are reductionist and oversimplified.
- There may be a genetic influence, but social factors are also important.
- Plomin (1990) argues for a genetic effect in the form of an absence of a control mechanism.

Personality characteristics

Substance abuse may be related to personality. Flory et al. (2002) found alcohol abuse was more common in extroverts. McAdams (2000) linked alcohol abuse with low levels of conscientiousness. According to psychodynamic theory, substance abusers have strong levels of dependency linked to early childhood (Shedler and Block, 1990). A child whose needs are not satisfied by parents may become over-dependent as an adult and use drugs as substitute comfort. Antisocial personality disorder (APD) has been found to be associated with several forms of substance abuse (Fabrega et al., 1991).

APD (antisocial personality disorder) a condition where a person lacks empathy and conscience

Study: Morgenstern et al. (1997)

Morgenstern et al. used interviews to establish personality characteristics and patterns of alcohol abuse with abusers attending a treatment centre. Traits typical of APD were found to be associated with alcohol abuse.

Evaluation

- Various traits are linked to abuse and some evidence is contradictory.
- Establishing cause and effect is impossible in correlation studies.
- Most personality research is restricted to alcohol abuse.

Examiner tip
Use your knowledge of social psychology from Unit 2 to answer questions on social factors and peer influences. Specialist terms such as conformity, compliance, internalisation and normative influence can aid your discussion.

Social factors and peer influences

Social learning, role models, peers, social norms and sociocultural factors may be involved in substance abuse. Social learning occurs through observation, imitation, modelling and vicarious reinforcement. We are more likely to imitate models that are similar and high status. For alcohol abuse, role models tend to be parents; for cannabis and cocaine abuse, role models are usually peers (Stein et al., 1987).

Study: Garnier and Stein (2002)

Garnier and Stein conducted a longitudinal study from when mothers were pregnant until 18 years later when their children were teenagers. Substance abuse in teenagers was significantly associated with substance abuse by peers.

The relationship between peer influence and behaviour is complicated because peer groups are part of a wider subculture with its own norms and values.

Norms of acceptable behaviour differ across cultures and subcultures, for example levels of alcohol abuse are linked to whether or not drunkenness is socially acceptable (Helzer and Canino, 1992).

Evaluation

- High self-efficacy can reduce social and peer influences (Bandura, 1997).
- Although drug use may be due to social influences, drug abuse may be more related to personal factors (e.g. genetics, personality).

Treatment and prevention

Summary specification content

Psychological treatments and their effectiveness, including aversion therapy and self-management.

Prevention techniques. Identifying and targeting 'risk' groups. Use of fear-arousing appeals. Social inoculation.

Health promotion/education in treatment and prevention. Stages of behaviour change proposed in the Prochaska model.

Psychological treatments and their effectiveness

Aversion therapy

Aversion therapy is based on classical conditioning. An abused substance is paired with an unpleasant stimulus (e.g. electric shock or emetic). After several pairings, the person becomes classically conditioned to fear or avoid the substance. Rapid smoking is a form of aversion therapy used to stop people smoking (Danaher, 1977). Covert sensitisation therapy is a form of aversion therapy involving the association of unpleasant thoughts or images with the substance. Covert sensitisation seems to be effective for alcohol abuse and in helping to stop smoking (Emmelkamp, 1996).

Study: Wiens and Menustik (1983)

Wiens and Menustik treated a large sample of alcohol abusers with aversion therapy involving an emetic drug. Over 60% stopped drinking alcohol in the year after therapy and 30% remained alcohol-free for 2 years.

Evaluation

- Success with aversion therapy is limited and often short term.
- The person must be motivated and needs support to cope with withdrawal.
- It can be successfully combined with other therapies, e.g. biological therapy.
- Aversion might be seen as unethical, although people must give consent.

> **Examiner tip**
> Be clear about the difference between prevention and treatment. Prevention means stopping a person from beginning to abuse a substance. Treatment is about stopping the abuse when it has already started.

> **Examiner tip**
> Use a classical conditioning diagram to help explain the process of aversion therapy. Remember, the unpleasant substance (e.g. emetic) is the UCS and the abusive substance (e.g. alcohol) is the CS.

- It has been used most with alcohol abuse and smoking. Behavioural treatments based on operant conditioning (e.g. contingency training) may be more effective for other substances.

Study: Higgins et al. (1993)

Higgins et al. used contingency training to treat cocaine abusers. They received incentives (lottery tickets) if their urine sample indicated they had not taken cocaine. After a 6-month programme, 68% were drug-free for at least 8 weeks.

Self-management

Self-management involves monitoring intake and gaining insight into the causes and consequences of abuse. Alcoholics Anonymous (AA) is one example. Moos and Moos (2004) found regular AA attendance helped people to stop drinking.

Self-management can be community-based, for example the North Australia Coast Study for smoking led to a 30% reduction over 3 years.

Study: Botvin et al. (2001)

Botvin et al. used a community programme in inner-city schools with a large sample of teenagers. Information included the negative effects of binge drinking. Binge drinking was reduced in the programme compared to a control group.

One successful self-management strategy is cognitive behaviour therapy such as behavioural self-control training (Miller et al., 1992). Alcohol abusers use a combination of insight and practical techniques to self-manage their problem, leading to 70% improvement. The approach has also been successful with people who abuse cannabis and cocaine (Carrol and Rounsaville, 1995).

Evaluation
- Many groups do not keep records, so evaluation is difficult.
- Programmes vary enormously.
- Better programmes incorporate help to resist peer pressure.

Prevention techniques

Primary prevention is about preventing substance abuse starting. Secondary prevention is aimed at those at risk. Tertiary prevention is focused on preventing those already abusing from developing further problems.

Identifying risk groups

Naidoo and Wills (1998) identified three risk factors:
- psychosocial (e.g. unemployment, social isolation, poor housing)
- cultural (e.g. Gray et al. (2000) found a risk of alcohol abuse in Aboriginal Australians)
- biological (e.g. family history)

Knowledge check 39

Identify two treatments for substance abuse that are based on behavioural principles.

Examiner tip

Explaining the difference between primary, secondary and tertiary prevention and the implications of these types of prevention might be useful in discussion.

Drug Action Teams (DATs) combine the efforts of social services, the police, education services and health professionals to target young people at risk.

Study: Drummond (2002)

Drummond investigated the role of accident and emergency (A and E) health workers in targeting alcohol abusers. People identified through A and E were invited to attend an advice clinic. Approximately 50% attended and discussed their problem.

Evaluation

- It is important to consider social and cultural problems and not just to focus on the individual.
- Drugs workers should be sensitive to people's circumstances.
- Identification of high-risk groups requires coordination of services.

Fear-arousing appeals

Fear-arousing appeals involve the use of shocking media messages or images to deter people from substance abuse. Janis and Hovland (1959) identified three key factors:
- source factors (e.g. expertise, trustworthiness and status of the source)
- message factors (e.g. type of message — high or low fear)
- audience factors (e.g. intelligence, self-esteem)

Baumeister and Covington (1985) found the effects of a fear appeal are more long-term in people with high self-esteem.

Study: Janis and Feshbach (1953)

Janis and Feshbach used high, medium and low fear appeals in lectures on tooth decay. Strong fear appeal caused most anxiety and was rated as most interesting but led to the least behaviour change. Low fear appeal caused least anxiety in the audience but resulted in greatest behaviour change.

Evaluation

- Flay (1985) found fear appeals were not effective for smoking prevention.
- High fear messages may lead people to 'switch off'.
- Fear appeals are indiscriminate and not aimed at specific groups.
- Fear appeals compete with advertising campaigns that portray substances as desirable (Borum, 2000).

Social inoculation

Social inoculation involves training in resistance to persuasion and changing attitudes and behaviour. Flay et al. (1985) identified four key elements:
- knowledge about the negative effects
- discussion about the roles of peers etc.

risk group a group of people whose characteristics, situation or lifestyle make them more likely to become substance abusers

Examiner tip
Be able to explain how fear appeals might be used by giving detailed, practical suggestions with information about the medium (e.g. film, image, story), the shock content and the target audience.

Knowledge check 40
Explain why high fear messages may be less effective than moderate/low fear messages.

- skill development to resist and deflect peer criticism
- public commitment to not take or abuse

Study: McAlister et al. (1980)

McAlister et al. used social inoculation techniques with teenagers. They learned and rehearsed arguments about why they should not smoke. Over a number of years they were less likely to smoke compared to a control group.

Evaluation

- Social inoculation helps people resist social pressure.
- Programmes are best delivered by someone similar to the target group or of high status.
- Cuijpers et al. (2002) found social inoculation in Dutch schools led to reduced alcohol use but increased cannabis use.
- Little research has been carried out with older people.

Health promotion/education in treatment and prevention

Health promotion uses four main methods:
- information giving (e.g. about medical conditions linked to substance abuse)
- information to motivate — to make the person want to be healthy
- motivational interviewing — usually one-to-one
- behavioural techniques — to replace unhealthy behaviours with healthy ones

Campaigns can take place at school, at work or in the community.

Study: Moher et al. (2005)

Moher et al. reviewed the effectiveness of work-based attempts to help employees to stop smoking. Some programmes focused on individuals (e.g. counselling, nicotine replacement). Others were aimed at the whole workforce (e.g. bans, incentive schemes). Strategies aimed at individuals were more effective.

The Prochaska model of behaviour change

Prochaska et al. (1992) proposed a six-stage spiral model of behaviour change. The model acknowledges that people do not always succeed in changing their behaviour at first. The six stages are as follows:
(1) pre-contemplation — person is not aware of problem
(2) contemplation — person is aware of problem and has started to think about changing
(3) preparation — person has decided to change behaviour soon
(4) action — behaviour changes for at least 1 day
(5) maintenance — behaviour change is maintained for 6 months
(6) termination — new behaviour is now 'normal' and relapse is unlikely

Knowledge check 41

What are the four stages of social inoculation training for resistance of peer pressure?

Examiner tip

Information on health promotion/education can be used in answers on both treatment and prevention.

Examiner tip

Knowledge of the Prochaska model can be used in discussing treatments. For example, someone in the action or maintenance stage would be most likely to present for treatment whereas someone in the earlier stages would probably resist treatment.

Evaluation

- There is a high rate of success with programmes based on this model.
- The structure reduces a difficult task into manageable steps.

Knowledge check 42

What are the six stages of behaviour change proposed by Prochaska?

- Physical dependence — the body needs the substance in order to function normally.
- Psychological dependence — the belief that the substance is necessary.
- Tolerance — the body adapts to the substance, meaning more is required for the same effect.
- Withdrawal — unpleasant physical/psychological side effects when use of the substance is stopped.
- Nicotine is a stimulant. A biological explanation for nicotine dependence is the nicotine regulation model. Alcohol is a depressant. Stimulants increase the activity of the CNS. Depressants slow down the activity of the CNS.
- The hereditary explanation for alcohol abuse suggests a genetic predisposition.
- Substance abuse has been linked to personality characteristics, e.g. extroversion and APD.
- Social factors affecting substance abuse include modelling, peer pressure, norms and culture.
- Psychological treatments include aversion therapy, covert sensitisation, contingency training and self-management e.g. AA.
- Prevention techniques include identification of risk groups, fear arousal and social inoculation.
- Health promotion/education can help in either prevention or treatment.
- The Prochaska model of behaviour change describes a cycle: pre-contemplation, contemplation, preparation, action, maintenance, termination.

Summary

Forensic psychology

Offending behaviour

Summary specification content

Problems in defining crime. Measuring crime, including official statistics and alternatives (victim surveys and self-report measures). Offender profiling, including typology and geographical approaches.

Theories of offending. Early biological approaches: atavistic form and somatotype theories. Biological explanations, including genetic transmission, Eysenck's theory of the criminal personality. Psychodynamic and social learning theory explanations.

Problems in defining crime

Factors such as historical context, culture, age of offender and specific circumstances all make it difficult to define crime.

- When — what was once a crime may no longer be a crime and vice versa.
- Where — a crime in one culture may not be elsewhere.
- Who — in the UK the age of criminal responsibility is 10 years.
- What — some 'crimes' are committed with good rather than bad intent.

Knowledge check 43

Give an example of something that used to be a crime in the UK but is no longer a crime.

Measuring crime

Three ways of measuring crime are official statistics, victim surveys and offender self-reports.

Content Guidance

Official statistics

These consist of reported and recorded crime. Hollin (1992) estimated these account for only 25% of crime. The 'dark figure' of crime is those offences that are not included in official statistics. Differences in police recording rules may affect recorded crime in different areas.

Study: Farrington and Dowds (1985)

Farrington and Dowds analysed records of crimes in Nottinghamshire and two neighbouring counties. They found Nottinghamshire police recorded crimes under £10 value whereas the other forces did not, distorting official figures.

Victim surveys

People are asked if they have been a crime victim, such as in the **British Crime Survey (BCS)**, conducted biennially.

For the 2006 BCS a large sample of 47,000 people, plus a booster sample of 4,000 16–24-year-olds, was interviewed using a structured interview. The BCS results showed an overall crime increase of 3% compared to official figures, which showed an overall decrease of 2%.

Self-report measures — offender surveys

These involve asking offenders to report their offending behaviour. Self-report surveys focus on people previously convicted and other groups known to be at risk of offending.

The Offending, Crime and Justice Survey (OCJS) involves interviewing 10–25-year-olds about antisocial behaviour (e.g. shoplifting) and drug use. It is a longitudinal study as the same people are interviewed over time. The 2006 survey showed that alcohol was a key factor in offending.

Evaluation

- The 'dark figure' of crime is neglected in official statistics.
- Victim survey data is based on retrospective reporting.
- Offender self-reporting assumes honesty.

Offender profiling

Offender profiling is used to predict personality or behavioural characteristics of an offender based on analysis of the crime. Initially used by the FBI, it allows investigators to narrow down the field of possible suspects.

The typology approach

Interviews with 36 sex offenders in the USA led to a belief that sexually motivated murderers and some arsonists could be classified as organised or disorganised offenders (Douglas et al., 1992). Organised offenders plan the offence, target a stranger and leave little evidence. They tend to be socially competent, in a skilled job

Examiner tip

When describing official statistics you must emphasise that these are based on crime that has been reported (for example by a witness or victim) and recorded (by the authorities i.e. the police).

British Crime Survey (BCS) a national survey of all aspects of crime, including a victim survey, attitudes to crime, fear of crime and detection rates

Examiner tip

In your answers you need to make the distinction between victim surveys and offender surveys absolutely clear. They are quite different.

AQA(B) A2 Psychology

and living with a partner. Disorganised offenders do not plan, know the victim and leave evidence. They tend to be socially inadequate, unskilled and living alone.

Study: Canter et al. (2004)

Canter et al. analysed data from 100 murders for characteristics typical of either organised or disorganised offenders. They found evidence for the existence of a subset of organised characteristics in most serial killers, but concluded that no subset of disorganised characteristics existed and therefore the disorganised type had no validity.

Evaluation

- The distinction is based on a small sample.
- A third category, 'mixed' offender, was added later.
- Modern personality theory suggests behaviour is not consistent across different situations, conflicting with the idea of a typology (Alison et al., 2002).

Knowledge check 44

What is meant by an 'organised' offender?

Geographical approaches

Geographical approaches involve inferring the offender's base on the basis of crime locations (Rossmo, 1997) and assume that offenders like to operate in familiar areas. Canter and Gregory (1994) found many offenders have a crime range of only 2 miles. Geographical profiling is based on schema theory about the mental representation of information. An offender's mental map determines where his or her crimes are committed and knowledge of this enables investigators to predict the offender's base and typical everyday movements, narrowing down the search area.

Study: Canter (1986)

Canter profiled the Railway Rapist (John Duffy), who was responsible for sexual assaults and murders in London. Using geographical information and witness reports, Canter's remarkably accurate profile led to Duffy's arrest. The profile correctly predicted where Duffy lived, that he was separated and worked on the railways.

Study: Lundrigan and Canter (2001)

Lundrigan and Canter used information from solved murder cases, analysing distances between the offender's home and body disposal locations. They found that the offender's home was often geographically central to disposal sites and that disposal often followed a predictable pattern.

Evaluation

- Geographical approaches are based on memory theory (schema theory).
- They can be used for different types of crimes, including burglary.
- Geographical information alone is insufficient. Other information such as crime scene behaviour, timing and nature of the victim are also relevant.

Examiner tip

When discussing geographical profiling it is helpful to place your answer in the context of theory about how we memorise places (spatial schema).

Evaluation of offender profiling

- Pinizzotto and Finkel (1990) tested five groups on their ability to construct profiles for a previously solved murder and sex offence. Trained profilers produced more accurate profiles for the sex case but not for the murder.
- Profiles contribute to identification in few cases (Pinizzotto, 1984)
- 70% of police officers questioned its usefulness (Bartol, 1996).

Theories of offending

Early biological approaches

Lombroso's atavistic form

Lombroso (1876) argued that offenders were a separate species, a primitive genetic form (atavistic). He noted that convicts had distinctive physical anomalies (e.g. large jaws, extra hair) and proposed that they were born criminals.

Sheldon's somatotype theory

Sheldon (1949) proposed three different body shapes or constitutions: endomorphs, ectomorphs and mesomorphs. He suggested that the muscular mesomorph was the criminal constitution, showing aggressive traits.

Study: Sheldon (1949)

Sheldon rated photographs of delinquents and controls on a scale of 1–7 for mesomorphy. The average rating was 4.6 for the delinquent photos and 3.8 for the controls.

Evaluation

- Goring (1913) found little evidence of atavistic features in a large sample.
- Criminality became associated with ethnic groups possessing atavistic-type features.
- The idea of a criminal stereotype is rooted in Lombroso's theory.
- Sheldon did not use the legal criteria for delinquency and rated the photographs himself.
- People with certain features and build may be expected to be aggressive, leading to a self-fulfilling prophecy.

Biological explanations

Genetics

An early study of criminal concordance by Lange (1929) found identical (MZ) twin rates of 77% and non-identical (DZ) twin rates of 12%, suggesting criminality is inherited.

AQA(B) A2 Psychology

Study: Grove et al. (1990)

Grove et al. investigated concordance in MZ pairs separated soon after birth. Each was interviewed in adulthood and scored for psychiatric disorder and antisocial personality. The rate of concordance for antisocial personality disorder was 29%, suggesting that antisocial traits were partly genetic.

Study: Mednick et al. (1984)

Mednick et al. studied adopted children in Denmark, comparing their criminal conviction rates with those of their biological and adoptive parents. Of those with criminal biological parents, 20% had convictions. The rate was 13.5% in those with no biological history of criminality.

Chromosomes

Criminality was once linked to the atypical sex chromosome pattern, XYY (Jacobs et al., 1965). However, Witkin et al. (1976) found very few cases of XYY in a huge sample and this theory of offending is no longer accepted.

Neurophysiology

Certain brain structures (limbic system and amygdala) control aggression in animals. People with antisocial personality disorder (APD) show abnormal EEG patterns, indicating brain immaturity which may explain impulsive, self-centred behaviour.

Study: Raine et al. (2000)

Raine et al. used scans to measure brain volume in people with APD and controls. An 11% reduction in grey matter was noted in the prefrontal area for APD participants.

Evaluation
- Even MZ pairs are not 100% concordant.
- Early twin studies were unreliable (e.g. they were not always properly determined as MZ or DZ, not always separated).
- Criminal behaviour of biological parent and child may be due to inherited mental disorder rather than inherited criminality.
- Biological explanations are reductionist and oversimplified.

> **Examiner tip**
> When discussing biological explanations for offending, try to give a range of different explanations, not just the genetic explanation.

Eysenck's theory of the criminal personality

Eysenck (1964) suggested our inherited nervous system dictates our personality and that people vary across two principal dimensions: introvert-extrovert (IE) and neurotic-stable (NS). He later added a psychoticism (P) dimension (cold, heartless). Eysenck suggested that the criminal type is the neurotic-extrovert. Extroverts have a chronically under-aroused nervous system that leads them to seek sensation; they are not easy to condition so cannot learn from mistakes. Neurotics are emotionally unstable and unpredictable.

Study: McGurk and McDougall (1981)

McGurk and McDougall compared Eysenck's Personality Inventory (EPI) scores for delinquents and non-delinquents. They found the delinquent group showed higher P, E and N scores than the controls.

Evaluation

- Not all research indicates high E scores in delinquent populations.
- More recent personality theories suggest other traits may be important.
- Moffitt (1993) suggests there are different types of offenders, not just one.
- The theory is testable and the EPI has good reliability.

Psychodynamic explanations

Superego

superego part of Freud's three-part personality that acts as an internal parent or conscience

The **superego** is internalised through identification with the same-sex parent in the phallic stage. It is the internal parent or conscience. Blackburn (1993) suggested offending may be due to:

- a weak superego (the child has not identified and has no moral code)
- a deviant superego (the child identifies with an immoral parent)
- an over-harsh superego (the child misbehaves to fulfil an unconscious desire for punishment and guilt)

Maternal deprivation

Bowlby (1951) used evidence from animal studies and his study of 44 juvenile delinquents to propose that maternal deprivation in the first 2 years may lead to delinquency and affectionless behaviour.

Defence mechanisms

Defence mechanisms can explain crime in various ways, for example an offender may use denial (refusing to consciously acknowledge the seriousness of a crime) or sublimation may be used where an offender carries out a lesser (less unacceptable) crime instead of a more serious one.

Evaluation

- Unconscious processes cannot be tested empirically.
- Most people who grow up without a same-sex parent do not offend.
- Bowlby's research was retrospective and the theory much criticised.

Social learning explanations

Social learning theory (SLT, Bandura, 1977) predicted that offending is learnt through observation, imitation and vicarious reinforcement (learning through seeing the consequences for others). Sutherland (1939) proposed differential association theory. He suggested offending is learnt through association with peers, family etc. whose values we adopt. Sutherland argued that if offenders receive reinforcement (approval) from others for criminal behaviour, the behaviour will be repeated.

Study: Farrington (2006)

In a longitudinal study of boys in a deprived area, Farrington recorded details of background, parenting and criminal convictions. Over 40 years, 41% of participants had criminal convictions. Criminal family history and poor parenting were key factors, supporting learning theory explanations.

Evaluation

- Learning explanations contrast directly with biological explanations.
- Poor socialisation is linked to crime but may not be the cause.
- Family history may support biological rather than social explanations.

Knowledge check 46
Explain what is meant by differential association theory.

Dealing with offenders

Summary specification content

The role of custodial sentencing. Effectiveness of custodial sentencing, including recidivism. Alternatives to custodial sentencing.

Treatment programmes: behaviour modification and anger management.

Evaluation of these treatment programmes.

The role and effectiveness of custodial sentencing

A custodial sentence is a prison sentence. The aims of custodial sentencing are:
- incapacitation — offending cannot continue while in prison
- rehabilitation — reform of the offender into a better person
- retribution — society 'gets its own back'
- deterrence — putting the offender (and others) off committing further crime

Examiner tip
Understanding these four aims is important because you can use them to discuss custodial sentencing and its alternatives, and the different treatments for offending.

Study: Zimbardo et al. (1973)

Zimbardo et al. studied the effects of imprisonment in a role-play experiment. Student volunteers were randomly allocated to roles of 'prisoner' or 'guard' in a role play to last 14 days. 'Prisoners' quickly became passive and submissive. 'Guards' abused their power, subjecting 'prisoners' to punishments. The research was stopped after 6 days because of prisoner anxiety and distress.

Evaluation

- Davies and Raymond (2000) concluded that custodial sentences primarily serve the purpose of retribution.
- Recidivism (re-offending) rates of approximately 75% in young males suggest custodial sentences do not reform or deter (Cullen and Minchin, 2000).
- Prison has many negative effects, including institutionalisation, psychological disturbance, brutalisation, loss of family contact and lowered employment prospects.

Alternatives to custodial sentencing

You need to be able to describe and evaluate two alternatives to custodial sentencing, such as antisocial behaviour orders, electronic tagging, community service or restorative justice.

Electronic tagging

Electronic tagging involves fixing an electronic device to an offender's ankle, enabling continuous monitoring of his or her movements and reducing the chance of further offending. Tagging can aid in the supervision of curfew orders where the court says an offender must remain at home during certain hours (usually during the evening). The tagging system was introduced in 1999.

Study: Cassidy et al. (2005)

Cassidy et al. studied juvenile offenders aged 12–16 years. They found tagging was used mostly with repeat offenders and that young males and black males were over-represented in the population. Tagging was found to lead to a 7% decrease in breach of bail conditions. The researchers concluded that tagging can be effective.

Evaluation

- Electronic tagging is cheap compared to custodial sentencing.
- It can be an effective alternative to custodial sentencing in helping prevent offending.
- Offenders can maintain family ties.
- The negative effects of prison can be avoided.

Restorative justice

This usually involves meetings between offender and victim, allowing the offender the opportunity to make amends and see the suffering the crime has caused. Restorative justice emphasises psychological healing and collaboration. It can also involve practical reparation (an offender giving something back in practical terms). It can be used alongside other forms of sentencing or on its own.

Study: Sherman and Strang (2007)

Sherman and Strang analysed studies comparing restorative justice and conventional punishments. Programmes varied but included victim–offender meetings and financial restitution. They found restorative justice resulted in reduced recidivism. For victims, desire for revenge and stress were reduced.

Evaluation

- Victims often do not want to meet the offender.
- Restorative justice can be seen as an easy option.
- Programmes vary so much that evaluation is difficult.
- Drop-out rates tend to be high.

Examiner tip
Remember to discuss these alternatives to custodial sentencing in the light of the aims of punishment: incapacitation, rehabilitation, retribution and deterrence.

restorative justice a relatively new approach to dealing with offenders where the offender and victim meet and the offender is encouraged to make amends

Knowledge check 47
What is the difference between primary reinforcers and secondary reinforcers?

Treatment programmes

Behaviour modification

Behaviour modification involves reinforcing desirable behaviour and extinguishing undesirable behaviour using operant conditioning. In prison this normally involves a token economy.

Study: Cullen and Seddon (1981)

Cullen and Seddon used a token economy in a youth offenders' institution. Positive behaviours were rewarded and undesirable behaviours were not. Those taking part demonstrated more positive behaviours during the study.

Evaluation

- Token economies have ethical problems.
- They may lead to 'token learning' (superficial). Blackburn (1993) argued there is no real change.
- Benefits are mostly short term, although Cohen and Filipczak (1971) found that recidivism was reduced for at least 2 years.

Anger management

Anger management programmes focus on understanding and controlling anger. Novaco (1985) identified three stages:

(1) cognitive preparation — the offender learns to recognise anger and situations that cause anger
(2) skill acquisition — techniques to control anger are taught, e.g. relaxation and self-talk
(3) application practice — new techniques are practised, e.g. in role play

Study: Ireland (2000)

Ireland studied group anger management over 12 hour-long sessions. Anger levels were assessed before and after the programme period. In the programme group, 92% showed improved anger levels on at least one measure. The researchers concluded the programme was effective.

Evaluation

- Anger management programmes are effective in the short term and make prisoners more manageable.
- They focus on changing understanding, not just behaviour.
- Anger may not be the cause of offending (Loza and Loza-Fanous, 1999).
- Offenders must be motivated to change.

token economy
a system of rewarding desired behaviour with secondary reinforcers (tokens) that can then be exchanged for primary reinforcers (e.g. food, telephone calls, entertainment)

Examiner tip
Descriptions of anger management should be in concrete terms. Answers that refer simply to 'learning to control anger' do not attract credit. You need to explain exactly what happens.

Knowledge check 48
What are the three stages of anger management?

Content Guidance

Summary

- Historical context, culture, age of offender and circumstances make it difficult to define crime.
- Crime measures include official statistics, victim surveys and offender self-reports.
- Offender profiling: using information about the crime, scene and victim to predict the personality/characteristics of the offender. The typology approach: organised and disorganised offenders. The geographical approach: memory theory and crime location to predict the offender's base.
- Early biological approaches: Lombroso's atavistic form and Sheldon's mesomorph.
- Later biological explanations: genetic theory of inherited predisposition; XYY theory; abnormal brain structure/function; Eysenck's criminal personality.
- Psychodynamic theory: dysfunctional superego; maternal deprivation; defence mechanisms.
- Social learning theory: observation, imitation, modelling and vicarious reinforcement. Differential association theory — offending depends on association with those who have criminal norms and values.
- Aims of punishment: incapacitation, rehabilitation, retribution and deterrence. Recidivism rates question the effectiveness of custodial sentencing. Zimbardo: negative effects of prison.
- Alternatives to custodial sentencing: tagging and restorative justice.
- Treatments for offending: behaviour modification (operant conditioning) and anger management (cognitive therapy).

Questions & Answers

In this section of the guide, there are eight questions, one on each topic. Each question is worth 20 marks. You should allow 40 minutes when answering each question.

This section is structured as follows:
- sample questions in the style in which they appear on the Unit 3 examination paper
- analysis of each question, explaining what is expected in each sub-section of the question
- example student responses at the C/D-grade level (student A) — these have been selected to illustrate particular strengths and limitations
- example student responses at the A-grade level (student B) — such answers demonstrate thorough knowledge, a good understanding and focus on the questions

Examiner's comments

All student responses are followed by examiner's comments. These are preceded by the icon. They indicate where credit is due and, in the weaker answer, they also point out areas for improvement, specific problems and common errors such as poor time management, lack of clarity, weak or non-existent development, irrelevance, misinterpretation of the question and mistaken meanings of terms. The comments also indicate how each example answer would be marked in an actual exam.

The examination

The Unit 3 examination is 2 hours long and you have to answer on three topics: one on child development and two on applied options. Each topic carries 20 marks, so you should allow 40 minutes for each topic in the examination.

All questions are structured, which means that there are several subsections to each topic. The first subsections are usually short-answer questions worth 1, 2, 3 or 4 marks. These are followed by a final subsection that requires extended writing for 12 marks.

Short-answer questions

- Commands such as 'identify', 'state', 'name' 'suggest' and 'give' require only the briefest of answers.
- Questions that contain commands such as 'outline' and 'describe' require descriptions.
- Verbs such as 'explain' and 'distinguish' indicate that analysis or elaboration is required. In the case of 'distinguish', you need to explain the difference(s) between two concepts.
- The command 'briefly discuss' requires description and evaluation or criticism, and is usually worth 4 or 5 marks.
- If asked to 'describe a study' for 4 marks, you should refer to the aim, method, results and conclusion.

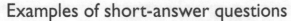

Examples of short-answer questions

- Identify two stages of moral reasoning proposed by Kohlberg.
- Explain what is meant by *labelling* in relation to schizophrenia.
- Give two consequences of rejection.
- Outline what psychologists mean by conservation.
- Describe one study in which eyewitness identification procedures were investigated.
- Briefly discuss one limitation of behaviour modification as a treatment for offending.
- Distinguish between problem-focused and emotion-focused strategies for stress management.

Long-answer questions

These are worth 12 marks. A typical 12-mark question would ask you to 'describe and evaluate' a theory, an explanation or some research. In 12-mark questions, there are 4 marks for description and knowledge and 8 marks for evaluation/analysis/application. In the evaluation, you should present strengths and limitations. If relevant, you should support what you say with reference to evidence and explain how the evidence relates to the topic. You can also get evaluation marks by comparing — for example, introducing an opposing theory to illustrate the limitations of the theory you are discussing. You should aim to spend plenty of time on this subsection of the question in the examination.

In the 12-mark questions you will be assessed on your ability to communicate. You should make sure that your answer is properly structured into sentences and paragraphs, and pay attention to spelling. If a 12-mark question asks you to 'refer to evidence' or 'refer to an alternative explanation', there will be a limit to the number of marks that you will be awarded if you do not comply with that instruction.

Mark schemes for 12-mark questions are banded into 'very good', 'good', 'average to weak' and 'poor' bands. This means that the examiner will not only consider each individual point that you make, but will also make a global assessment of the answer as a whole. Students who show extensive knowledge and make lots of evaluation points but who do not present a well-argued response will sometimes be awarded a lower mark than they might have been given. This is because the answer as a whole is better suited to the 'good' band than to the 'very good' band.

Scenario questions

In some questions, you must use your knowledge by applying what you have learned about psychology to a novel situation. For example, a question might include a scenario about two people who show different responses to a stressful situation. In this case, you might be required to use your knowledge of stress to explain the experiences or behaviours of the people in the scenario.

Assessment of practical psychology and research methods

In Unit 3, your knowledge of practical psychology and research methods will be tested in the context of the child development questions. For example, there may be a cognitive development question in which you are asked about a study of cognitive development that has been described to you. In this unit, questions on research methods and practical psychology will be restricted to the content of research methods in Unit 1 and what you have covered through your own practical exercises in class. You will not be expected to know about inferential statistics, statistical tests or the issues in the research section of Unit 4.

It is therefore important that you reread and revise the research methods section of Unit 1 before you take the Unit 3 examination.

Assessment objectives

Examination boards use the term 'assessment objective' (AO) to refer to the different types of skills that you might be expected to demonstrate in examinations. Your teacher might have told you about AO1, AO2 and AO3 skills:

- AO1 refers to knowledge and understanding.
- AO2 refers to analysis and evaluation and the application of knowledge to novel situations.
- AO3 refers to knowledge and understanding of research methods and practical psychology.

In most cases the wording of the question will lead you to demonstrate the necessary skills. Only the following two types of question require you to think about AO skills:

- 'Describe and evaluate', 'discuss' or 'compare' for 12 marks: whatever the wording of the 12-mark question, 4 marks are for description (AO1) and 8 marks are for evaluation, analysis and application (AO2).
- 'Briefly discuss' for 3, 4 or 5 marks: here, there would normally be 1 or 2 marks for description (AO1) and 2 or 3 marks for evaluation, analysis and application (AO2).

Child development

Question 1 Social development

(a) In a study of children's friendship, a researcher compared stories written by 5-year-old girls and 5-year-old boys about their 'best friend'. Working alone, she categorised each story as either 'intimacy-focused' or 'activity-focused'.
(i) Use your knowledge of research into children's friendships to propose a suitable research hypothesis for this study. (2 marks)
(ii) Identify one methodological limitation of this study. (1 mark)

℮ For a 2-mark hypothesis in part (i), you need a testable statement in which the variables are clearly specified. Part (ii) requires only the briefest answer. In cases like this, where the description of the study includes a limitation, you would not get marks for proposing another possible, but unknown, limitation. For example, if you said that the type of sample was a limitation, you would not get any credit because we are not told anything about the sample.

(b) (i) Describe one effect of institutionalisation. (3 marks)
(ii) Briefly discuss the effect you have identified in your answer to part (i). (2 marks)

℮ In part (i) you should describe one relevant effect in some detail. Be careful not to fall into the trap of giving several different effects — this would be a waste of time. In part (ii), you need to offer some evaluation or analysis. A couple of brief points or one issue in a bit more detail will suffice.

(c) Discuss Bowlby's work on attachment. (12 marks)

Total: 20 marks

℮ You need to show fairly concise knowledge of Bowlby's work as there are only 4 marks for description/knowledge. The other 8 marks are for evaluation/analysis, i.e. presenting strengths and limitations and using evidence to support what you say. In this context 'work' could refer to theory and also to research.

Student A

(a) (i) There is an association between the sex of the child and the story they write **a**.

℮ 1/2 marks awarded **a** Here the student correctly predicts an association between the variables, gaining 1 mark. The independent variable is sufficiently specified by the word 'sex' as this could only mean whether the children are male or female, but the dependent variable is not clearly defined. Had the student explained the two possible outcomes for the story (activity-based or intimacy-based), this would have been worth the full 2 marks. Note that a hypothesis worded in terms of differences between numbers of males and females would also be credit worthy.

(ii) One limitation with the study is the boys and girls might have different views about friends, even if they are the same age **b**.

ⓔ **0 marks awarded** The student has not realised the basic flaw in the study. **b** This answer is hinting (not very well) at a possible confounding variable and, in any case, is confused.

(b) **(i)** One likely effect is developmental delay **a**, meaning a child has lower cognitive ability than non-institutionalised children of the same age. Reading and language ability would all be slowed if the child lives in an institution and there may be evidence of poorly developed social skills etc **b**.

ⓔ **3/3 marks awarded a** This answer gives one effect and **b** expands on it sufficiently.

(ii) The delay effect depends on what facilities and toys there are and not just on where they are etc **c**.

ⓔ **1/2 marks awarded c** The critical comment is briefly explained but not fully explored. It certainly looks as if the student knows the answer, i.e. the effect is more likely to be due to the impoverished environment in some institutions than on the institutionalisation itself. Often, students assume examiners will 'fill in the rest' but it really is up to the student to make the point.

(c) Bowlby was famous for saying that mother love is as important as vitamins and that children who did not have mother love would grow up to be damaged and violent **a**. He interviewed teenagers in a juvenile detention centre who had been separated from mothers and noted how they were more likely to be delinquent as teenagers **b**. However, we do not know if they really remembered being separated **c**. Bowlby filmed children whose mothers went into hospital and found that they often could not get back with their mother. They would not look at her and found it difficult to trust people **d**.

At the time Bowlby was speaking about his theory, not many people went to nursery. These days they do and they are not all damaged psychologically, so it is unlikely that his theory is relevant nowadays. Also, many people who are not separated from mothers do not grow up to be thieves and so there must be other reasons. In praise of Bowlby, it was good that he drew attention to childhood experience as important for future health and behaviour **e**.

ⓔ **5/12 marks awarded** This is quite a brief answer. **a** The basic idea of long-term consequences is worth AO1 credit and **b** there is just enough description of the 44 thieves study for further credit. The point that follows **c** is meant to be a criticism of the study, but it is insufficiently explained. Here there should be a full explanation of how the data was retrospective and therefore unreliable. **d** The student gets confused about the Robertson studies; Bowlby did not carry out the research. However, the basic point that this is further evidence in support of Bowlby's views is worthy of credit. **e** The final paragraph is also creditworthy. Although a little anecdotal (phrased in everyday terms) and poorly argued, these are reasonable points and add to the discussion. This answer is fairly typical of the average-to-weak band (AO1 = 2, AO2 = 3). Total for this question: 10/20 marks — approximately Grade D.

Student B

(a) (i) There will be a difference in the numbers of boys and girls writing activity-based stories and intimacy-based stories **a**.

ℯ 2/2 marks awarded a Here the hypothesis is testable and includes reference to both variables, so the student gets full marks. It would have been nice to see a directional hypothesis as research into friendship would allow for a prediction that boys' friendship is more about shared activity and girls' friendship is more about intimacy. However, the hypothesis here is technically correct and testable.

(ii) One problem is lack of reliability. The researcher is the only person categorising, so she might be subjective **b**.

ℯ 1/1 marks awarded b This is a good answer that is straight to the point.

(b) (i) One effect might be developmental delay **a**, which means retarded development. Institutionalised children often have cognitive problems, e.g. poor reading.

ℯ 2/3 marks awarded a An appropriate effect is given but the description/elaboration is limited.

(ii) Evidence for this effect was demonstrated by the ERA group research with Romanian orphans. Rutter thought that adoption could overcome the negative effects. However, this seems to be possible only if a child is adopted before 6 months of age **b**.

ℯ 2/2 marks awarded The discussion is brief but well done. **b** Evidence (the ERA research) is used effectively here, first to support the effect given and then in reference to Rutter's original position and the counter-argument.

(c) Bowlby was known for his theory of maternal deprivation. He stated that children should have a warm and uninterrupted bond with a single person, usually mother, for the first 2 years or else they would be delinquent and have other negative effects. Bowlby believed that children have an innate desire to stay close to this one figure, which helps them survive. He was a psychoanalyst and his evidence came from studying monkeys and 44 juvenile delinquents. These were boys Bowlby studied retrospectively using interviews with them and their parents. He found that many of them recalled they had been maternally separated and 17 eventually showed affectionless behaviour. He thought that if the attachment was broken or delayed in the critical 2 years, the damage would last for ever **a**.

Critics of Bowlby say he confused deprivation with privation, which was actually what happened to the monkeys who had no mother at all when they were infants. Privation is never having had a bond, whereas deprivation is when you have a bond and then it is broken. According to Rutter, privation is much more severe than deprivation. At least if a child has had chance to form a bond at some time, he or she has some idea of loving relationships and does not grow up to be an affectionless psychopath **b**.

Another problem for Bowlby is that other researchers showed how children do not have one single attachment and it does not have to be the mother. For example, Schaffer and Emerson in Glasgow found most children have multiple attachment figures, often including the father, and Freud and Dann found that seriously traumatised, separated children can form substitute attachments. It has also been shown that even late adopted children can form satisfactory and loving attachments, as in the case of the deprived Koluchova twins whose adult relationships were normal and happy **c**. Bowlby's study of juvenile thieves was also retrospective and therefore not sound evidence — it is likely that the boys' recall of childhood events was not reliable **d**.

ⓔ **11/12 marks awarded a** The first paragraph is a concise yet detailed account of the main points of Bowlby's work. Although the terms 'monotropy' and 'critical period' are not used explicitly, these ideas are clearly described. There is reference to the negative effects of deprivation, innate desire for proximity and the 44 thieves study. Although Harlow's research is mistakenly attributed to Bowlby, the content of the first paragraph nevertheless scores the full credit. In the next paragraph **b**, the student thoroughly explores the point about confusion between deprivation and privation; the terms are clarified and the difference in consequences for future relationships is explained. In the final paragraph **c**, the student argues against the focus on the mother, monotropy and the critical period, using counter-evidence effectively. **d** The final brief point about the 44 thieves study is just sufficiently elaborated for further credit. Note that had this student not already gained the maximum AO1 marks for knowledge, he or she could have been awarded 1 mark for description of evidence here. The discussion is awarded 7 out of 8 AO2 marks and the answer as a whole fits the top-band descriptor (AO1 = 4, AO2 = 7).

Total for this question: 18/20 marks — Grade A

ⓔ **Consistent performance at this level would merit an A* grade providing other A* requirements are met.**

Child development
Question 2 Cognitive development

(a) Two groups of children were asked to solve a puzzle by fitting 30 shapes together. One group of children performed the task alongside an adult, who made helpful suggestions at the start and then gradually withdrew support. Another group of children performed the task alone. One week later, all the children were tested on their ability to solve a similar puzzle alone.
  (i) What influence on cognitive development is being investigated in this study? (1 mark)
  (ii) Identify the independent variable in this study. (1 mark)
  (iii) Suggest one measure that could be used as the dependent variable. (1 mark)
  (iv) Identify the experimental design in this study. (1 mark)

ⓔ All parts require only the briefest answer. You do not even need to write in full sentences if you know the correct term/name.

(b) Outline and briefly discuss the information processing approach to cognitive development. (4 marks)

ⓔ You have to provide an outline, which is just a brief description, and then offer some discussion point (evaluation or comment). This could be one elaborated point or a brief mention of two points.

(c) Describe and evaluate Piaget's theory of cognitive development. (12 marks)

Total: 20 marks

ⓔ This looks like a dream question because every student knows a lot about Piaget's theory. However, remember that there are only 4 marks for knowledge and description of the theory; the remaining 8 marks are for evaluation. A common error in a 12-mark Piaget question is to spend too long on description and run out of time for discussion or evaluation. Note that the question is asking you to describe and evaluate the theory and not the evidence. In a 12-mark question, you can usually gain one AO1 mark for describing a relevant study, but do not describe lots of studies in detail here.

> ### Student A
>
> **(a) (i)** Problem-solving is being studied **a**.

ⓔ **0 marks awarded a** The student has not understood the key difference between the two conditions and therefore gains no marks.

> **(ii)** The independent variable is the support that is given or not given **b**.

ⓔ **1/1 marks awarded b** The independent variable is correct despite the mistake in part (i), so 1 mark is awarded.

> **(iii)** They could record how long it takes put the shapes together **c**.

ⓔ **1/1 marks awarded c** This is a good idea, which gains 1 mark.

> **(iv)** Independent measures different in each condition and not matched **d**.

ⓔ **1/1 marks awarded d** It would be enough to simply name the design here.

> **(b)** The information processing approach suggests that cognitive development is about the amount of ability increasing with age, e.g. memory gets more efficient with age. Bee says that with age children use better strategies because they have better metamemory **a**.

2/4 marks awarded **a** This answer is awarded 2 marks for the outline but there is no discussion. This is a fairly common mistake in 'Briefly discuss…' questions.

(c) Piaget's theory was a stage theory. There are four stages, from birth until 12 years when schema have fully developed. At each stage thinking was different. In the sensori-motor stage, children are egocentric and do not have object permanence. If a toy is covered they will not carry on and look for it. In the pre-operational stage, children are still egocentric but now have object permanence. They cannot do the three mountain task because they cannot see another's point of view. They cannot conserve either. In the next stage, they can conserve so can tell that a long, thin glass holds the same as a short, fat glass. They can do class inclusion tasks, but at this time they can only reason about real things and cannot do abstract reasoning and hypothesising about 'what would happen if…' This arises in the formal operations stage when the child can do abstract thought **a**.

Piaget has been criticised for his methods because he did most experiments himself with his own children. He did not have proper controls or use statistics. Others have copied his work and found different results. For example, Bower turned out the lights; Hughes did a different egocentrism experiment and the results were different. Children aged 3 or 4 could put the doll where the policeman could not see him, showing they did not have egocentrism **b**.

ⓔ **6/12 marks awarded** The student has realised the problem here and tried to trim the content down to a manageable size. **a** The first paragraph is a description of Piaget's stage theory. Each stage is noted and the student correctly shows the basic characteristics of thinking at each stage. Although it is not well written, there are no errors and most key concepts (e.g. egocentrism and object permanence) are briefly explained. It is a shame that there is not more on general aspects of Piaget's theory, such as adaptation and schema development, but this would have been a lot to expect in such limited time. The full 4 marks are awarded for AO1. **b** In the second paragraph, several evaluation points are presented. The methodological criticisms could have been expanded with an explanation of why these issues are a problem and how they might have affected Piaget's conclusions. The alternative research and findings could have been compared to Piaget's work in much more detail. For example, why was Hughes able to demonstrate that 3- or 4-year-old children were not egocentric when Piaget did not? In all, this paragraph is credited for the methodological points and for the very brief noting of alternatives. Overall, the answer appears to be at the top of the average-to-weak band (AO1 = 4, AO2 = 2).

Total for this question: 11/20 marks — approximately Grade D/C

Student B

(a) **(i)** The researcher is studying scaffolding **a**.

ⓔ **1/1 marks awarded a** This answer gains 1 mark.

(ii) The independent variable is whether the child has the support of scaffolding or not **b**.

ⓔ I/I marks awarded **b** The independent variable is correct and the student specifies both conditions.

> **(iii)** The number of shapes fitted together in 1 minute **c**.

ⓔ I/I marks awarded **c** This is a plausible idea. The student gets I mark.

> **(iv)** Independent design **d**.

ⓔ I/I marks awarded **d** I mark is awarded for a correct answer.

> **(b)** Information processing theorists see children's thinking as similar to computer processing **a**. This is a problem in child development because children develop in a social context and are active in their problem-solving. Children might also solve problems in novel or unusual ways, which a computer could never do **b**.

ⓔ 3/4 marks awarded **a** I description mark (AOI) is awarded for a sensible point about information processing theory. Unfortunately, this has not been expanded by further description. **b** The discussion is brief but relevant and well applied to children's thinking, so worth 2 AO2 marks.

> **(c)** Piaget was an influential theorist whose ideas, such as discovery learning, have been much used by classroom teachers **a**. His stage theory explored the development of thinking and described how children's schemas develop from being simple, motor schemas into an abstract understanding. He believed that due to active experience, knowledge adapts through assimilation and accommodation. In the sensori-motor stage, a baby has no object permanence, meaning he or she cannot understand that an object continues to exist when it is out of sight. In the pre-operational stage, there are many constraints. The child is egocentric and thinking is ruled by outward appearance so the child cannot conserve volume, mass etc. In the concrete operational stage, these abilities are developed, the child can imagine another's point of view and can use logic with concrete problems. In the final stage, there is abstract, hypothetical reasoning **b**.
>
> Piaget's ideas about active experience and readiness to learn have been criticised by people who argue that sociocultural influences such as friends, family, peers and teachers affect cognitive development and that it can be accelerated. Vygotsky did not agree with Piaget that the child was like a scientist or sole explorer. Instead, he saw the child as an apprentice to the skills and knowledge of his or her culture **c**. Other researchers claimed that Piaget underestimated children's abilities because he always assumed that failure to perform a task meant that the child was unable to perform it. Critics thought Piaget's theory was based on misinterpretation of the results of his studies. For example, in conservation experiments Piaget asked a child the same question twice, perhaps leading them to assume the first answer was wrong, so explaining the second incorrect answer. In short, Piaget himself was egocentric, failing to see his experiments from the point of view of the child **d**.

AQA(B) A2 Psychology

Although Piaget's ideas are much used in education, they can lead to problems. If teachers always waited for a child to be ready to learn, some children would never progress. Also, children left to discover things on their own may not have enough structure to their lessons and may waste a lot of time. However, Piaget is to be acclaimed as a key figure in child development **e**.

🅮 **12/12 marks awarded** This is an excellent balance of description and evaluation. **a** The student starts well by making a simple evaluative comment about educational application of the theory. This gains AO2 credit. **b** The rest of the first paragraph is a concise account of the main aspects of the theory, including key concepts and detail of the stages. Note there is no description of evidence. As there is ample descriptive material without detail of studies, it would have been a waste of time in this case. The student gains 4 AO1 marks for knowledge of the theory. In the second paragraph, he/she makes two creditworthy points in the first sentence. **c** The comparison with Vygotsky is a useful way to gain more analysis/evaluation marks. **d** The points about underestimation, misinterpretation and Piaget's own egocentrism are relevant and well expressed and the example of conservation is used to maximum effect. **e** The final paragraph is interesting and unusual as students usually tend to assume Piaget's ideas always had a positive effect on education. This student usefully presents some potential negative implications of the theory, returning to his or her first point about education. In all, this is a knowledgeable and well-argued answer with insightful evaluation. The maximum 8 AO2 marks are awarded (AO1 = 4, AO2 = 8).

Total for this question: 19 out of 20 marks — Grade A

🅮 **Consistent performance at this level would merit an A* grade providing other A* requirements are met.**

Child development

Question 3 **Moral development**

(a) **Children hear a story about Ed, who has the chance to help his classmate tidy up the classroom. If Ed stays behind to do the tidying, he will miss having chocolate biscuits at playtime. Children are asked individually whether Ed should help and, if so, why. Use your knowledge of Eisenberg's theory of moral reasoning to:**
    (i)   **Identify the type of moral dilemma facing Ed.**   (1 mark)
    (ii) **Give one likely response of a child in the hedonistic stage. Explain your answer.**   (2 marks)
    (iii) **Give one likely response of a child in the approval stage. Explain your answer.**   (2 marks)

🅮 Part (i) requires the briefest answer. In parts (ii) and (iii), you have to suggest a possible response and explain how that response demonstrates hedonistic or approval-oriented reasoning.

(b) **Briefly evaluate the moral comparison technique.**   (3 marks)

ⓔ This is a methodology question where you need to evaluate a method of studying moral development. Here you could choose one issue and expand on it in some detail or you could consider more than one issue in less depth. Whichever approach you take, be careful not to spend too long on this question as it is worth only 3 marks.

(c) Discuss Gilligan's work on moral development. (12 marks)

Total: 20 marks

ⓔ This is a straightforward question where you are looking for 4 AO1 marks and 8 AO2 marks. This means you should aim to spend more time on discussion than on description. The question asks about 'Gilligan's work', which means both theory and research. Although there is no explicit requirement for you to make comparisons with alternative views, this is often a good way to get evaluation marks.

Student A

(a) **(i)** Ed has to decide whether he should hurt the other child's feelings. This is his dilemma so morally he might be worried that he will get punished for not helping the boy **a**.

ⓔ **0 marks awarded a** The student has attempted an answer but has not recognised that this is a prosocial dilemma, so no mark is given.

(ii) A child in the hedonistic stage might say 'Ed should not help' because he would miss the biscuits, which is all he thinks about, what he wants **b**.

ⓔ **2/2 marks awarded b** The likely response is appropriate and there is just about enough explanation for full marks. It would have been better if the student had explained fully what hedonistic meant, but it is implied here.

(iii) A child in the approval stage would say 'Ed should help' because it would be nice of him **c**.

ⓔ **1/2 marks awarded c** Again, this is an appropriate response. However, the explanation is not really adequate because there is no direct reference to the most important aspect of the approval stage, i.e. that other people would think well of him.

(b) In the moral comparison technique, Piaget asked children to listen to two stories and then to choose who was the naughtiest person in the stories. In one story a little boy called John knocked over one cup on purpose and in another Henry smashed 15 cups by mistake. Most children under the age of 7 chose Henry because he had caused the most damage. Older children tended to choose John because he did it on purpose. Alternatively, the younger children maybe could not remember the stories well **a**

AQA(B) A2 Psychology

e **1/3 marks awarded** Although this student clearly knows a lot about the technique, the content is almost entirely descriptive; **a** there is a single brief evaluation point at the end, almost like an afterthought. This answer is awarded only 1 mark, although the student probably thought he or she had answered it well.

(c) Gilligan studied women having abortions at a clinic, which was a good thing to do because it was a real-life dilemma, not hypothetical, and therefore had high ecological validity **a**. She found they showed stages of reasoning. Some women focused only on what they wanted: this was self-interest. Others thought that the needs of other people were most important, like the baby or the father. This is sacrificing. This led Gilligan, who was a woman, to propose the ethic of care which is a description of female moral reasoning **b**. She was a student of Kohlberg and thought he was biased in favour of males and therefore she said that women and men reasoned differently (care or justice) but that one was not any better than the other, unlike Kohlberg who thought men reasoned at a higher level **c**.

Gilligan's view was good because, until her work, the study of moral development had been looking just at male morality, e.g. Kohlberg's research. However, some have argued that she too was biased because she only studied women. If she had asked men about abortion, she might have found that they reasoned a bit like women when it comes to such a sensitive issue. Walker said this was the case **d**.

e **6/12 marks awarded a** The first point about ecological validity is a sensible one and gets AO2 credit. **b** The description that follows shows some knowledge of Gilligan's work. There is confusion over the three levels (not two stages) and the names given here are not exactly correct. The answer gains 3 rather generous AO1 marks for content that is slightly inaccurate and lacking in detail. **c** At the end of the first paragraph, AO2 credit is awarded for the comparison with Kohlberg. **d** In the second paragraph, there is further comparison with Kohlberg and a valid point about the relevance of the type of the dilemma. Indeed, this is what Walker found, although the student does not offer any further information about Walker's study, which could have gained more marks, either AO1 for description or AO2 for analysis of what the results showed in relation to Gilligan's work. This is a respectable average-to-weak band response (AO1 = 3, AO2 = 3).

Total for this question: 10/20 marks — approximately Grade D

Student B

(a) (i) This is a prosocial dilemma **a**.

e **1/1 marks awarded a** This is a clear answer.

(ii) A hedonistic child would say Ed should not help. Instead, he should be hedonistic and do what is most pleasurable for him, i.e. have the chocolate biscuits **b**.

e **2/2 marks awarded b** A clear and well-explained answer that is worth full marks.

(iii) An approval stage child would say Ed should help because then the teacher would think he was a good person and praise him **c**.

(e) **2/2 marks awarded c** This is another sound answer that deserves full marks.

(b) The original moral comparison technique (John and Henry and the cups) was used by Piaget. It requires reasoning about who is more naughty in a hypothetical situation. The big problem with how Piaget did the experiment was that he varied the amount of damage and whether the damage was on purpose or not at the same time. This means he had two independent variables and did not really know which one influenced the children's decisions. This was a basic flaw in his design. Nelson did a variation where she used four stories, which improved the technique **a**.

(e) **3/3 marks awarded** This is a direct answer. **a** The student chooses an issue, the problem of manipulating two variables, and explains it thoroughly enough for full marks.

(c) Gilligan did not agree with Kolhberg that female reasoning was less sophisticated than male reasoning. She suggested that women had an ethic of care which led them to focus on care for others and empathy. In contrast, men had an ethic of justice which led them to focus on justice and the law. She argued that this is the reason females were often at Kohlberg's level three and males at level four. In short, she argued Kohlberg's system was male-biased **a b**.

In her own research, Gilligan studied 29 women considering abortions using structured interviews **b**. This method means everyone gets the same questions and therefore there is less researcher bias. As this was a real-life dilemma, this research has high ecological validity which is an improvement on the hypothetical dilemmas used by other researchers **c**. Gilligan found three types of reasoning. The least sophisticated was self-interest where women only thought about themselves ('It will ruin my life.') This is similar to Kohlberg's reward stage reasoning or Eisenberg's hedonistic reasoning **d**. In the self-sacrifice stage, women think only about others like the unborn baby, their partner etc. In the most sophisticated stage, non-violence, they try to consider all points of view and the main concern is with not hurting anyone **b**.

This research has been criticised though. Perhaps Gilligan should have studied men's view on abortion too. Indeed, Walker found that the type of reasoning depended on the type of dilemma. Walker's research showed that both men and women can use justice-based and care-based reasoning in different situations. This means Gilligan's views on ethic of care and ethic of justice were perhaps over-simplified **e**.

Gilligan and Freud both argue there are differences between male and female morality. However, Gilligan would not agree that females are morally inferior, as Freud stated **f**.

(e) **12/12 marks awarded** This is a well-constructed answer that **a** starts with a comparison with Kohlberg that gains AO2 credit. **b** In the first and second paragraphs there is sufficient knowledge for 4 AO1 marks. The concepts of ethic of care and ethic of justice are clearly outlined, the stages are correctly named and outlined and there is some description of the abortion clinic study. **c** The evaluative points about real-life versus hypothetical dilemmas and the structured interview are embedded in the description of the Gilligan study. Although there is no requirement to integrate evaluation and description, it does make the answer flow better and appear more sophisticated overall. **d** Note how the student gains more AO2 credit by quickly comparing Gilligan's levels with those of Kohlberg and Eisenberg. **e** In the third paragraph, the student explores Walker's criticism of Gilligan's conclusions, gaining more AO2 credit. **f** In the last paragraph, there is a neat comparison with psychodynamic theory, giving both a similarity and a difference. Although not a long answer, there is sufficient evaluation, analysis and comparison for the top band (AO1 = 4, AO2 = 8).

Total for this question: 20/20 marks — Grade A

ⓔ **Consistent performance at this level would merit an A* grade providing other A* requirements are met.**

Applied options

Question 4 **Cognition and law**

(a) Using your knowledge of psychology, outline and briefly discuss one way in which children's ability to recall events differs from that of adults.   (4 marks)

ⓔ There are 2 marks for an outline and 2 marks for a brief discussion or evaluative comment. Note that only one difference in recalling events is required, so if you gave more than one you would be credited for the best. However, this would be a waste of time, so it is not an advisable strategy. The question refers to 'knowledge of psychology' so the answer should have some basis in research or theory.

(b) Identify and briefly explain two implications of the false memory debate.   (4 marks)

ⓔ Often, students answer questions like this rather vaguely, letting the two points get muddled together. Then there is a danger that the examiner will spot only one of them. To be sure, you should separate the two implications clearly. Start with 'The first implication is…' and then, on a new line, 'The second implication is…'.

(c) Discuss one way of improving eyewitness recall. Refer to evidence in your answer.   (12 marks)

                                                                                Total: 20 marks

ⓔ Your answer must focus on one way of improving recall. It is legitimate to refer to other possible ways as part of the discussion, as long as you do not lose sight of the focus of the discussion. Note the specific requirement for evidence here. If you do not refer to any studies,

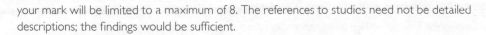
your mark will be limited to a maximum of 8. The references to studies need not be detailed descriptions; the findings would be sufficient.

Student A

(a) Children make up things more than adults because they have such good imaginations. This means that their recall of events is sometimes unreliable **a**. It is also found that children's memories are more distorted through talking about it afterwards **b**.

ⓔ **2/4 marks awarded** The first sentence is anecdotal, **a** but fortunately there is a reference to lack of reliability in the second sentence. This basic point gains 1 mark. **b** In the next sentence there is a brief point about the influence of post-event discussion, which could easily have been expanded. As it is, this gains a further mark.

(b) One implication is that at least judges and professionals are aware that some of the recovered memories may not actually have happened. We should not always assume it is a true account of the child's past **a**. Another implication is that families can be destroyed. There would be no going back from that **b**.

ⓔ **2/4 marks awarded a** The first implication is valid and coherently explained, so worth 2 marks. **b** The second point is much briefer and there is no clear link to the debate. This point is not sufficiently explained for credit.

(c) One way to improve eyewitness recall is by restoring the context. People remember more when they are in the same context as when they learned the information **a**. This was done by Baddeley in the underwater study, where people who learned either on land or underwater and then had to recall either on land or underwater were found to recall more of the nonsense words if they were in the same place where they first learned them **b**. However, this study is not ecologically valid because it is unlikely a person would witness something and then be in the same place when they recall it. They would probably be in a police station. Also, eyewitnesses have more important information to recall than nonsense words, so there is more pressure on them to recall than there was on the divers **c**. Restoring the context could be done by asking the witness to imagine what they felt like at the time **d**. This is done in the cognitive interview and results show it leads to much better recall compared with normal interviews (Geiselman) **e**.

Another way to improve recall would be to make sure the witness does not talk to anyone after the event because then there would be less post-event contamination **f**. Of course this would mean keeping the person in isolation, so in practice this is not going to be a helpful way of improving recall. Another way is to use modern composite systems for constructing faces rather than the old-fashioned identikit system **f**. Modern systems such as VIPER do not have crude lines between features and can be adjusted slightly to get the best likeness.

ⓔ **6/12 marks awarded a** This answer starts well and gets AO1 credit for outlining restoring context as an appropriate way of improving recall. **b** The evidence is probably a study that was covered in the AS year but is relevant here and is properly described, so worthy of AO1 credit. **c** There is an evaluative comment about ecological validity. Students often use this term but do not get credit because they fail to explain what they mean in relation to the study presented. This student gives well-elaborated explanations and gains substantial AO2 credit. **d** There follows a valid point about how context can be restored in the cognitive interview, which gains AO1 credit and, finally, **e** a brief reference to findings in relation to effectiveness for AO2. **f** In the following paragraph, the student gives two additional ways of improving recall. Unfortunately, these receive no credit because the question specifies just one way. In this case, the examiner has credited whichever material benefits the student more. (AO1 = 3, AO2 = 3).

Total for this question: 10/20 marks — approximately Grade D

Student B

(a) One difference is that adults get less confused about where their memory comes from. This is known as source monitoring. Adults tend to remember better whether something really happened to them or whether they heard about it **a**. This is shown in the Mr Science study where children thought they had seen science demonstrations they had only heard about. However, in real life children have to remember much more important things (e.g. abuse) than in studies **b**.

ⓔ **4/4 marks awarded** This is a comprehensive answer. **a** Source monitoring is named and fully explained, with the difference between adult and child recall made absolutely clear. **b** For discussion, the student has used evidence to back up the point and then offered a critical comment about the evidence. This answer deserves full marks.

(b) One implication is that Loftus's theory of reconstructive memory may not be right **a**. Another implication of the debate is ethical. If memories are often false, as Loftus argues, then some cases of 'recovered memory' where people accuse parents of childhood abuse may not really be recovered memories at all. In which case, parents might be convicted when they did not do anything **b**.

ⓔ **3/4 marks awarded** This student separates the two implications and offers one theoretical and one ethical. **a** The theoretical implication is not really explained at all, **b** but the ethical point is more detailed. The first point is awarded 1 mark and the second, 2 marks.

(c) One way of improving eyewitness recall is to use the cognitive interview. This is a special technique devised in the 1980s and now used by specially trained police officers. It involves four strategies. The first is reinstating the context **a**. Context has been shown to aid recall, for example, Malpass and Devine asked participants to recall an act of vandalism and found that those who were told about the time and date showed better recall than a control group **b**. To restore a witness's context, they could be told the date and asked to remember how they felt that day. Another strategy involves recalling in a different order, going back in time rather than chronologically **a**. So the witness would be asked, 'What happened before that?' instead of 'Then what happened?' Another strategy is asking about events from another perspective **a**, for example asking what a person on the other side of the room might have seen. Finally the witness should give the smallest details, even when they might seem unimportant **a**. Tiny details might overlap and lead to more important information. Of course, not all police officers would have the training to interview in this way, so the cognitive interview cannot always be used **c**.

Geiselman (1986) found that the cognitive interview technique led to more correct details being recalled, suggesting it is a highly effective technique **d**. However, others have disagreed that all four components of the cognitive interview are necessary. Milne found that the most helpful aspects were context and recalling all details, with the others less important **e**.

It also might work better in some situations than others. For obvious reasons, it is better for helping people recall events, where there is a sequence of things happening, than for aiding recall of faces. Face recognition seems to depend on many factors (top-down and bottom-up) and is a more complex process, so the cognitive interview is less helpful there **f**. Also, according to Freudian theory, witnesses to horrific events like car crashes might repress the detail into the unconscious. This would mean that the cognitive interview would not help access the memories. Horrific details that have been repressed might be more easily accessed through psychoanalysis **g**.

ⓔ **12/12 marks awarded a** There is detailed description of all aspects of the technique and reference to two studies. In this case, the description of the technique itself is worth the maximum AO1 marks, although, had it been presented in less detail, credit could have been awarded for evidence. In the first paragraph there are two creditworthy evaluative points: **b** use of evidence to support the point about the importance of context and **c** brief comment about not all officers being trained. Although this is not verified here, it is nevertheless plausible. In the second paragraph, **d** there is further use of evidence and **e** the point about the necessity to use all four aspects of the technique. Both these points are worthy of AO2 credit. In the final paragraph, **f g** two highly relevant points about face recognition and repression are discussed effectively, showing an impressively integrated understanding of the whole topic area. This paragraph is awarded substantial AO2 credit. Altogether, this response fits the description for a top-band answer (AO1 = 4, AO2 = 8).

Total for this question: 19/20 marks — Grade A

ⓔ **Consistent performance at this level would merit an A* grade providing other A* requirements are met.**

Applied options
Question 5 Schizophrenia and mood disorders

ⓔ The most important thing to remember in this question is to look carefully at each subsection before you start. Students often get mixed up and write about schizophrenia when the question subsection is about mood disorders or vice versa.

(a) (i) **Outline what is meant by bipolar depression.** (2 marks)
    (ii) **Briefly explain one problem that might arise when using cognitive therapy in cases of bipolar depression.** (2 marks)

ⓔ Part (i) requires a brief answer. The greatest risk here is confusion between bipolar and unipolar disorder. There are at least two valid answers to part (ii), which should be fairly obvious to those students who know that bipolar disorder involves bouts of mania and cognitive therapy involves reasoning and discussion. Students who are confused about either may struggle here.

(b) **Pat has been diagnosed as having schizophrenia. Her parents are very concerned.**
    (i) **Give two symptoms that Pat might be experiencing.** (2 marks)
    (ii) **With reference to labelling, explain the possible effect of diagnosis on Pat.** (2 marks)
    (iii) **Discuss biological and cognitive explanations for Pat's schizophrenia.** (12 marks)

Total: 20 marks

ⓔ In part (i), only the briefest answer is required. Part (ii) requires an understanding of the term labelling and the consequences of it. Again, only a brief answer is required. In part (iii), it is important to aim for an appropriate balance of knowledge and discussion. As usual in 12-mark questions, there is a maximum of 4 marks for knowledge, in this case of biological explanations, with the remaining marks for discussion, analysis and use of evidence. As always, it is possible to get at least 1 mark for knowledge of relevant evidence, although in this case it is unlikely that students will need to scratch around for extra AO1 marks. Although there is no instruction to compare biological explanations with alternatives, that would be another way to get AO2 credit.

Student A

(a) (i) Bipolar depression means the person goes between two extremes and is not just depressed **a**.

ⓔ **1/2 marks awarded a** The student conveys the idea of alternation, but fails to mention the mania end of the spectrum, so gets only 1 mark.

    (ii) Patients cannot be bothered with therapy. They are just too lethargic **b**.

ⓔ **0 marks awarded b** This is generally true of people with depression, but there is no attempt to answer in relation to bipolar disorder, so this answer is awarded no marks.

(b) (i) Two symptoms are catatonic rigidity and haphazard speech with words all in a jumble **c**.

ⓔ **2/2 marks awarded c** Full marks are awarded.

    (ii) Labelling is where you come to behave like the label because this is what other people expect **d**.

(e) **1/2 marks awarded d** This answer shows good knowledge of labelling, but it is not applied to Pat (e.g. by reference to how parents treat her) or schizophrenia and is therefore worth only 1 mark.

> **(iii)** There are many explanations for schizophrenia, including neurochemistry, which is because the dopamine is too high, and inheritance through genes. This is the biological explanation where they use identical and non-identical twins and find concordance rates are high for schizophrenia (Gottesman). This means that it must be biological. Other biologists have found that people with schizophrenia have enlarged fluid-filled brain cavities, which might cause their disorder **e**.
>
> In evaluation, the biological approach has a lot of evidence from different sources. They use twin studies and adoption studies and analyse brain chemicals, finding that patients with the disorder have different levels of dopamine to normal. Also, if animals are given dopamine they begin to show symptoms of the disorder such as catatonia **f**. However, these are animals and it may not be the same for people **g**. All this combined evidence leads to support for the biological explanation. Against the biological explanation is the idea that people who have recovered from schizophrenia will relapse if they go home to an over-emotional family. So it is not just biology that matters but also how you are treated **h**. The trouble with biological explanations is reductionism – it is too simple to explain something so complicated by chemical activity **i**.

(e) **6/12 marks awarded e** The first paragraph includes a reasonable outline of biological explanations — high dopamine, genetics and brain anomalies. This lacks detail, especially the genetic reference, so the AO1 content is not worth full marks, but there is limited knowledge of a range of biological explanations and **f** some weak knowledge of relevant evidence in the second paragraph. The second paragraph contains useful discussion; attempted use of evidence, **g** criticism of evidence, **h** an alternative explanation and **i** reductionism. Only the point about expressed emotion is properly developed. Had the student linked the evidence more thoroughly to the biological explanation and expanded on the issue of reductionism, this would have been a much better answer (AO1 = 3, AO2 = 3).

Total for this question: 10/20 marks — approximately Grade D

Student B

(a) **(i)** Bipolar depression is where the mood disorder is at both ends of the mood spectrum, with both depression and mania alternating **a**.

(e) **2/2 marks awarded a** This is a good answer, worthy of full marks. The idea of alternation between mania and depression is explicit.

> **(ii)** Bipolar patients become completely irrational and unreasonable in the mania phase. At this time they cannot have a sensible conversation, which would be necessary for cognitive therapy where the client and therapist have to work together to find solutions **b**.

ⓔ **2/2 marks awarded b** A good reason is given here and it is fully explained. This is a 2-mark answer.

(b) (i) Two symptoms are hallucinations and delusions **a**.

ⓔ **2/2 marks awarded a** Two correct symptoms gain full marks.

(ii) Labelling is where a person who has been diagnosed with a disorder starts to behave in the way expected of someone with that label **b**. Once Pat knows she has schizophrenia, she may start to behave in an even more disturbed way **c** and the label will come true — a self-fulfilling prophecy. This happened in Rosenhan's study when people were labelled with schizophrenia and people expected them to be odd and perceived odd behaviour even when they were doing normal things **c**.

ⓔ **2/2 marks awarded** This answer is easily worth full marks. **b** The definition is clear and **c** the answer is applied to schizophrenia through reference to 'disturbed' and 'odd' behaviour.

(iii) Undoubtedly schizophrenia has some biological component, although it would be an oversimplification to suggest the disorder is solely due to biology. Rather it is likely that biology predisposes individuals to develop the disorder, but that this predisposition is activated only under certain circumstances — this combination effect of genes and environment is commonly referred to as the diathesis-stress or interactionist approach. Most usually the external factor would be some stressful event, psychological or physical trauma **d**. This possibility will be explored later in the answer. First, let us address various biological influences that might explain schizophrenia.

Genetic evidence from both twin and adoption studies seems to support the view that schizophrenia is heritable. Gottesman (2001) reviewed many family studies, combining the data in a meta-analysis to show that the closer the genetic relatedness, the more likely there is to be concordance for the disorder. In twin pairs, for example, monozygotic pairs have 48% concordance whereas dizygotic pairs have 17% concordance **e**. This supports the view that schizophrenia has some genetic element although it could be argued that MZ have a more shared environment than DZs and this might account for their increased similarity **f**. Meta-analyses are useful for the amount of data yielded but not all studies are carried out under the same conditions, which might introduce unreliability **g**. Furthermore, since even identical twins with identical DNA do not show 100% concordance, there must be some environmental influence as well. In adoption research Tienara (1991) found people whose biological mother had the disorder were ten times more likely to suffer from schizophrenia than controls. Both twin and adoption evidence pointing in the same direction further suggests the robustness of the genetic hypothesis **h**.

Biochemistry research points to abnormal activity of dopamine in people with schizophrenia **e**. More recently this hypothesis has been elaborated to suggest that people with the disorder have increased sensitivity to dopamine, which explains some of the symptoms. The importance of dopamine is clear when we consider the mode of action of anti-psychotic drugs such as chlorpromazine, which block dopamine receptors, reducing activity of the chemical in the brain. These drugs, used since the 1960s, treat the most disturbing positive symptoms e.g. hallucinations. If blocking dopamine action eliminates the key symptoms it seems fair to assume that dopamine has some role in the symptoms and thus in the disorder. Critics would argue that, just because reducing dopamine treats the disorder, it does not necessarily mean that high dopamine activity was the cause in the first place. Although once the prevailing biochemical view, it now seems that other aspects of neurochemistry may be important e.g. serotonin may also be involved (Brier 1995) i.

Further biological evidence from scans shows sufferers have enlarged brain ventricles and differences in size/activity of the pre-frontal cortex, responsible for higher level thinking, e suggesting that biology might be responsible for the typical thinking disturbances (hallucinations, delusions) in schizophrenia j.

As with all biological explanations, there is a danger of reducing a highly complex disorder involving multiple symptoms to the malfunctioning of specific brain areas and neurotransmitters. To assume biology holds the key neglects the complexity of a disorder with many sub-types and varied symptoms. However, if biology does hold the key and we know exactly what imbalances are involved, then it may offer the possibility of treatment k. As stated earlier, perhaps we should consider biology predisposing to the disorder with social influences such as poor communication and high expressed emotion acting as triggers l.

Perhaps schizophrenia illustrates the competing influences of nature and nurture. We may be unlucky enough to inherit a predisposition in our genotype but manifest the condition in our phenotype only under certain environmental conditions, thus there is a biological explanation but this on its own may be insufficient to explain the disorder as a whole m.

@ 12/12 marks awarded Here description and discussion are integrated to produce a fluent and well-balanced answer. d In the first paragraph the student gains AO2 credit by setting the scene, introducing the biological explanation but noting how biology is only one aspect of the complex disorder. Notice the confident use of technical terms. e Knowledge of biological influences is evident in the second, third and fourth paragraphs with detailed references to genetics, twin evidence, dopamine and brain anomalies being ample for full AO1 credit. f g h In the second paragraph, there is use of evidence, evaluation of evidence and further discussion on genetics and reliability. In the third paragraph, i there is further AO2 credit through analysis of evidence in favour of the dopamine hypothesis and effective use of evidence. In the fourth paragraph, j further AO2 credit is awarded for analysis of the link between brain anomalies and symptoms. In the penultimate paragraph, k further AO2 credit is given for the issue of reductionism. Contrast the balanced discussion here with the simplistic approach to reductionism in Student A's answer. l At the end of this paragraph the issue of diathesis-stress is revisited, with comparison of social explanations as alternatives, for final AO2 credit. **m** The final analytical paragraph rounds the discussion off nicely and links back to the question for further AO2 credit with the link to nature–nurture.

Total for this question: 20/20 marks — Grade A

Consistent performance at this level would merit an A* grade providing other A* requirements are met.

Applied options

Question 6 Stress and stress management

(a) Daniel copes with the stress of work by going out and having a laugh with his friends. Bernie copes with the stress of work by seeing his supervisor and organising a reduced workload.
   (i) Distinguish between problem-focused and emotion-focused strategies. Refer to Daniel and Bernie in your answer. (5 marks)
   (ii) Bernie goes on a stress management course, where he takes part in biofeedback sessions. Outline biofeedback and suggest one limitation of the use of biofeedback for work-based stress such as Bernie's. (3 marks)

ⓔ Part (i) is asking you to do two things. First, explain the difference between problem-focused and emotion-focused strategies. The easiest way to do this is to define each, then to point out a difference. You then need to refer to Daniel and Bernie by explaining which type of strategy each is using. In part (ii), you need to provide a brief description of biofeedback and then briefly state one limitation. Note that this should not be a general limitation of biofeedback, but one that would apply where stress is related to work.

(b) Discuss the role of at least two personal variables in mediating responses to stress. (12 marks)

Total: 20 marks

ⓔ Here, there are 4 marks for knowledge and description of at least two personal variables, and 8 marks for discussion of their role in mediating responses to stress. The description marks should be obtained relatively easily as long as you choose relevant personal variables. As usual in the 12-mark questions, it is possible to get at least 1 description mark for knowledge of a relevant study. The discussion should focus on the role of personal variables in mediating stress, for example how they make it easier or harder for a person to cope in stressful situations. You could refer to evidence to support what you say and to alternative factors that might affect responses to stress. You would also be able to gain marks by evaluating the evidence you present.

Student A

(a) (i) Problem-focused gets to the heart of the problem, as Bernie is doing **b**. Emotion-focused is more about not dealing with it **a**. This is what Daniel is doing **b**.

(ⓔ) **3/5 marks awarded a** There is no clear definition of either type here, although an understanding of the difference is implicit. It is important to explain each point fully for maximum marks and, given that the answer is worth 5 marks, this student should have realised a more thorough answer was required. The answer gets 3 marks; **b** both strategies are correctly linked to Daniel and Bernie and a difference between them is briefly noted.

(ii) Biofeedback is where people get feedback about their body as they are doing a task. This allows them to control their body **c**. Bernie could then use this to deal with stress because when he feels his heart rate increasing he can cause it to be steady again and then not get upset.

(ⓔ) **1/3 marks awarded c** There is some understanding of the technique here, although the student does not make it clear that it is autonomic function that is being monitored or that reinforcement is involved. The student seems to have missed the second part of the question, as there is no suggestion as to why it would be difficult for Bernie to use biofeedback for work-based stress.

(b) Some people naturally have a personality that means that they can cope better with stress. These are type B personality as identified by Friedman and Rosenman. Type Bs are calm and laid back. They do not get upset easily and keep cool under pressure. On the other hand, type A people are the typical high-pressured executive types who get stressed easily **a**. They thrive on stress but eventually get burnt out by it and suffer from stress-related illness such as cancer and high blood pressure **b**. In a study to support this, Friedman and Rosenman measured stress in middle-aged men and found that the personality type could be used to predict whether or not they would develop high blood pressure. In fact, men identified as type A by their colleagues were five times more likely to develop heart disorders than type Bs **c**, so personality type affects response to stress **d**.

Another personal variable would be locus of control. This means how much you think you can control what happens to you **e**. It is much better to believe that we have high control over what happens and then we do not get so stressed out. This was claimed by Rotter and he used a questionnaire, the locus of control scale.

(ⓔ) **6/12 marks awarded** This student correctly identifies types A and B and describes each type. **a** The descriptions are a little anecdotal, but they are correct and therefore each is worthy of credit. **b** AO2 credit is awarded for explaining how personality type mediates the effects of stress, with type A being more likely to suffer stress-related illness. **c** At the end of the paragraph, there is a brief description of the study, which can be awarded further credit for description. **d** The findings of the study are used effectively for further AO2 credit. **e** In the second paragraph, another relevant variable — locus of control — is identified and outlined. It is a shame that the student does not use the terms internal and external and elaborate on how these two types of locus of control would mediate response to stress. No further credit is awarded as the student has not made it clear that a balance of internal and external is most healthy. This is fairly typical of an answer at the top of the average-to-weak band (AO1 = 4, AO2 = 2).

Total for this question: 10/20 marks — approximately Grade D

Student B

(a) **(i)** Emotion-focused strategies tackle the response to the stress rather than the stress itself. Problem-focused strategies tackle the source of stress rather than the person's reaction to it **a**. Daniel is using an emotion-focused strategy using friends as an emotional release, whereas Bernie's approach is to use a problem-focused way of sorting out the problem of workload **b**. Generally speaking, the problem-focused approach is more effective. It addresses the cause directly and doesn't simply involve putting off dealing with it **c**.

ⓔ **5/5 marks awarded** This is a full-mark answer. **a** There is clear knowledge of the two strategies and **c** the final sentence makes a clear distinction. **b** Each type is correctly explained in relation to Daniel's and Bernie's behaviour.

(ii) Biofeedback is a behavioural technique where patients are taught to monitor and control their own autonomic response (heart rate, muscle tension etc.) using reinforcement, for example when heart rate decreases back to normal **d**. A machine is necessary and it is difficult to do when relaxation is needed without the necessary equipment. This might not help Bernie when he is at work **e**.

ⓔ **3/3 marks awarded** This is a good answer. **d** There is ample description in the first sentence and **e** the student correctly identifies a problem — that the technique is hard to do without feedback and this would be impossible in a work situation.

(b) Not everyone responds to stress in the same way. One variable that mediates response to stress is hardiness, defined by Kobasa (1979) as a set of traits (commitment, control and challenge) that act as a buffer and enable a robust response to stress **a**. Challenge allows a person to see potential stressors as opportunities rather than threats **a**. This means that they see the positives to stress rather than just the negatives, so stress does not affect the person badly **c**. Commitment is in respect of family, job, community etc. A sense of control over events is also healthy as it enables the hardy person to feel he or she is effective and able to control life outcomes **c**.

Kobasa's research with 670 senior executives showed that those with high hardiness and high stress experienced less illness than those with low hardiness and high stress **b**. This supports the view that hardiness is a key factor in combating stress **d**. One problem with hardiness is that it may be a factor that occurs more in men than in women and therefore may mediate the effects of stress differently for males and females **d**. In addition, hardiness may not protect a person long term, as Rowe (1997) showed that even hardy people suffer from burn-out in jobs like social work **d**.

Neither is the relationship between control and stress straightforward. Rotter's work on locus of control showed how a balance of internal and external locus is most beneficial. It allows people to feel they have some control, but not to be so bound by control that they become distressed about things they cannot control **e**.

Another factor that mediates stress is personality type. Friedman and Rosenman found that people with a type A personality (competitive, self-critical and hostile) are more likely to suffer adverse effects of stress, particularly CHD, than type B who show broadly the opposite traits **f**. In their study, two groups of men, type As and type Bs, were compared. The type A men worked longer hours and had a family history of heart disease **b**. They showed how personality type was probably inherited and was linked to cardiovascular problems. Type As have since been found to show higher blood pressure, heart rate and stress hormone levels in response to stress **f**. Recently, a type C has been identified: a passive, emotionally suppressant person who deals with stress by denial (Holland and Lewis) **f**. This type has been related to risk of developing depression and cancer **f**. Although the idea of types A, B and C are generally accepted, it is now thought that hostility may be the key factor in response to stress **f**.

One problem with the personal variables mentioned is that they are usually assessed using self-report measures, which are not objective and therefore not scientific. In the case of personality type, however, behavioural measures are also taken, which allows researchers to cross-check for reliability **g**.

ⓔ **12/12 marks awarded a** The student gains all 4 description marks for accurate and detailed description of hardiness and personality types. **b** There is also description of two studies, which could have gained knowledge marks if there had not been sufficient material for full marks elsewhere. **c** In the first paragraph, AO2 credit is awarded for explanation of how two of the elements of hardiness mediate the effects of stress. **d** In the second paragraph, AO2 credit is awarded for use of evidence to support assertions about the role of hardiness and the analytical points about gender and long-term effects. **e** In the third paragraph, there is creditworthy analysis of the interaction between levels of perceived control and stress. **f** In the fourth paragraph, AO2 credit is awarded for analysis of how stress affects both type A and type C personalities and for the point about hostility. **g** The final paragraph gains further AO2 credit for discussion of the underpinning methods. This response easily fits the descriptor for the excellent band and deserves full marks (AO1 = 4, AO2 = 8).

Total for this question: 20/20 marks — Grade A

ⓔ **Consistent performance at this level would merit an A* grade providing other A* requirements are met.**

Applied options
Question 7 **Substance abuse**

(a) (i) **Describe how a youth worker might use social inoculation with teenagers as a way of preventing stimulant abuse.** (4 marks)

(ii) **Explain one strength and one limitation of social inoculation as a way of preventing substance abuse.** (4 marks)

(e) Part (i) assesses knowledge of social inoculation for preventing substance abuse and ability to transfer that knowledge to an applied situation. Start by outlining social inoculation and then explain how it might be used with teenagers at risk of stimulant abuse. It is important in these applied questions to make your idea for application as concrete as possible. In part (ii), you get 1 mark each for giving a relevant strength and limitation and a further mark each for elaboration (extended explanation saying how or why it constitutes a strength or limitation).

> **(b) Discuss hereditary factors as an explanation for substance abuse. Refer to evidence in your answer.**
>
> (12 marks)
>
> **Total: 20 marks**

(e) You need to describe hereditary factors and associated evidence for 4 marks, with a further 8 marks for discussion. This might include the use of evidence to support points, evaluation of the importance of hereditary factors and discussion of possible alternatives — note these must be presented in the context of the discussion to gain credit. Remember that, unless you give evidence, you will gain a maximum of 8 marks.

Student A

(a) **(i)** Social inoculation is where people have an inoculation process so that they can avoid abuse in a tricky situation. **a** This might involve role plays and modelling someone like a youth worker, who says 'No!' with assertive body language. **b** Another part of inoculation is group discussion about consequences.

(e) **3/4 marks awarded a** The first sentence is not worthy of any credit. **b** 2 marks are awarded for the second sentence, which gives a relevant aspect of the process and elaborates with an example. A further mark is given for another aspect of social inoculation in the final sentence, but there is no applied example.

(ii) A strength is that it works well **c**. It is better to inoculate people before they begin to abuse than to try to make them give up once they have started. An abuser can easily end up being physically dependent, which is harder to deal with **d**. A limitation is the cost. It would be expensive and where would the money come from? **e**

(e) **2/4 marks awarded c** Saying that a treatment or therapy 'works well' without any evidence to back up the statement is not worthy of credit. **d** The second point about prevention rather than cure is valid and well elaborated, for 2 marks. **e** The point about cost is a tricky one unless there is some attempt to quantify the costs or to compare the costs with other methods. No marks are awarded for the limitation.

(b) Inheritance means whether something is genetic, passed on in DNA from parent to child, in this case substance abuse **a**. Studies have been done with parents and children to see if they are both abusers **b**. This happens as has been found by Peters and Preedy, who showed 18% of alcohol abusers who were adopted had real parents with alcohol problems as well. This was not as much in the control group. Twin studies also show higher concordance rates in MZ twins than in DZ twins **c**.

Another cause of substance abuse could be personality, as extroverts were shown by Flory to be more likely to be substance abusers. This could be because they are always looking for excitement because their nervous systems are naturally low in arousal and they want more arousal **d**.

Psychodynamic psychologists believe that substance abuse is not genetic, but that it is due to upbringing. If children's needs are not met when they are little, they grow up to be always looking for comfort, and drugs and alcohol are a way of getting that substitute comfort. This cannot be inheritance but must be a result of experience and how people are treated **e**. Also, just because identical twins are similar for alcohol abuse that does not mean that the behaviour is inherited. Twins often grow up together and so they are treated more similarly, especially identical ones **f**.

e **4/12 marks awarded b** The student has missed several opportunities for gaining marks. Ideas are not always fully developed or not sufficiently linked to the question. **a** Credit is given for basic knowledge of hereditary factors in the first sentence. The reasonable description of Peters and Preedy earns more AO1 credit. It is a shame that the student did not explain how this evidence supports the role of hereditary factors to gain AO2 credit. **c** The sentence about twin studies is too general. There is nothing about substance abuse and no explanation of how the higher concordance in MZs might support a genetic explanation. **d** The paragraph about personality factors is irrelevant to the question — not used to discuss the hereditary explanation. In the final paragraph, the student appears to be making the same mistake again, as the first two sentences simply describe a possible alternative. **e** However, towards the middle of the paragraph, the student sets the alternative explanation against the role of hereditary factors, which is valid evaluation. **f** Further AO2 credit is awarded for discussion of problems with twin studies. In all, this is a weak average-to-weak band answer (AO1 = 2, AO2 = 2).

Total for this question: 9/20 marks — approximately Grade D/E

Student B

(a) **(i)** Social inoculation is giving people what they need to resist peer pressure to abuse. It normally involves four aspects: giving knowledge, discussion, skill development and public commitment **a**. In this case, you could get an expert to come to talk to the teenagers about the effects of stimulants. You could get mums of ecstasy users to join in a discussion about how the family is affected **b**. In a role play they could practise saying 'No' if ever a 'friend' asks them to join in with using ecstacy **b**. Finally, they could make 'No to ecstasy' wristbands and wear them every day for a week **b**.

e **4/4 marks awarded a** This detailed answer gets full marks. **b** The ideas for application are concrete, fully developed and relevant to the context. In fact, just two of these ideas would suffice for full marks.

(ii) One strength is that it has been found to be effective in the long term. McAllister showed how teenagers treated with social inoculation for smoking were much less likely to have taken up smoking years later **c**. A problem is that those delivering the programme should be similar to the target group or a high status celebrity for it to be effective. This means programmes delivered by ordinary youth workers may not be influential **d**.

🅮 **4/4 marks awarded** Both **c** strength and **d** limitation are valid and appropriately elaborated. Note how the student answers explicitly, making it clear which is the strength and which is the limitation. This answer is awarded full marks.

(b) Some types of substance abuse may be inherited, but most research in this area has focused on alcohol. Melo bred male and female rats that preferred alcohol to other liquids — the offspring of these pairs showed a preference for alcohol compared to controls. Thus it seems that alcohol preference at least is passed on from generation to generation **a**. However, preference does not necessarily equate to abuse. It could be possible to prefer alcohol over other substances but not to become an alcoholic. Still, this animal evidence does support a genetic component **b**.

Kaij (1960) investigated concordance rates for alcohol abuse in identical and non-identical twins and found a rate of 54% in identicals who share 100% of their genetic material. In comparison, for non-identicals who share only 50% of genes, the rate was 28% **a**. The higher rate for twins who share more of their genes strongly indicates a genetic component **c**. However, the concordance rate for identical twins is not 100% and therefore there must also be some environmental influence. Indeed, higher rates in identical pairs are just what environmentalists would expect due to the more shared environment of identical pairs. There are also problems with twin evidence as samples tend to be small **d**.

Adoption studies compare the behaviour of adopted children with that of their biological parents. Goldstein (1994) found that alcohol abusers who were adopted were more likely to have biological parents with an alcohol abuse problem **a**.

Gene-mapping techniques have linked a specific dopamine receptor gene to alcohol and cocaine abuse **a**, supporting the role of inheritance in substance abuse. As previously noted, most evidence relates to alcohol use and there is little evidence in relation to other substances **e**.

The usual position in relation to the effect of genetics on behaviour is that genes pre-dispose an individual, but the development of the condition may be triggered by factors such as stress **a**. Maybe people have the gene for substance abuse but do not always develop it because they do not experience the necessary trigger events. Plomin's view is different. He argues that alcohol abusers have genes that create an absence of brakes effect for control of alcohol intake, so people with this gene are unable to recognise when they should stop drinking **f**.

The role of inheritance in substance abuse may be complex. If personality types are largely inherited and some personality types, particularly antisocial, play a role in alcohol abuse, abusing may be inherited indirectly **g**. Morgenstern (1997) identified personality traits and patterns of alcohol abuse in 336 participants and concluded that APD is significantly associated with alcohol abuse.

A different approach to abusing is taken by those who believe that peer pressure and modelling affect whether or not someone abuses substances. Maybe genetic pre-disposition is a factor, but perhaps only those who are exposed to social pressure and inappropriate models develop substance abuse. Alternatively, perhaps people first use a substance because of social pressures, but only those with genes for abuse go on to develop full-blown abuse **h**.

e **12/12 marks awarded** **a** The student gains maximum AO1 credit for fully describing how inheritance may be involved in substance abuse. Evaluation, analysis and use of evidence are spread liberally throughout the answer. **b** In the first paragraph, the student explains the relevance of evidence from selective breeding experiments, gaining AO2 credit, making an insightful point about the difference between preference and abuse. **c** More credit is awarded where evidence from twin studies is used effectively. **d** Further AO2 credit is awarded for the discussion/evaluation of how twin study evidence should be interpreted and the reference to small samples. **e** The brief comment about research being largely restricted to alcohol abuse is worthy of credit as analysis. **f** The discussion about the interaction between genes and environment is given AO2 credit. **g** The clever analysis of the possible indirect inheritance of alcohol abuse via inherited personality is also awarded AO2 credit. **h** In the final paragraph, further AO2 credit is awarded for the alternative explanation and for discussion of how inheritance and social factors might interact. (AO1 = 4, AO2 = 8).

Total for this question: 20/20 marks — Grade A

e **Consistent performance at this level would merit an A* grade providing other A* requirements are met.**

Applied options

Question 8 **Forensic psychology**

(a) Outline and briefly evaluate one alternative to official statistics as a way of measuring crime. (4 marks)

e Here, 2 marks are available for knowledge/description of an alternative to official statistics and 2 marks are for a brief evaluation. These 2 marks can be gained by mentioning two evaluative points briefly or for expanding on one.

(b) A prison governor decides to set up a behaviour modification system in his prison. Explain what is meant by behaviour modification and how it might be used to treat offenders in a prison. (4 marks)

e In this section, 2 marks are for a brief description. Make sure you include the most important aspects of behaviour modification. The other 2 marks are for application to a prison situation. Make your ideas as concrete as possible and try to imagine exactly what would be possible in a prison. For example, using sweets as reinforcement might be appropriate if using behaviour modification in a primary school but not in a prison. In this sort of question, students often simply repeat the general description, adding words such as 'in prison' to try to make the answer applied. You need to make your suggestion practical by saying exactly what would happen.

> **(c)** **Many politicians argue that prison does not work and suggest that there are other, better alternatives. Discuss the effectiveness of custodial sentencing in the treatment of offenders. Refer to evidence in your answer.**
>
> (12 marks)
>
> **Total: 20 marks**

🅔 Start by outlining the role or aims of custodial sentencing. This is really describing what prison, or punishment more generally, is for and would be an easy way to get description marks. Description marks could also be awarded for knowledge of studies or factual information, for example recidivism rates. Having outlined the aims, you can then go on to determine whether or not these aims are being met and, if so, how effectively. For discussion, it is important to discuss recidivism, as one of the key aims of prison is generally thought to be reform. You might also refer to any negative consequences of custodial sentencing. The question mentions 'better alternatives', which seems to be inviting you to make comparisons. Use of evidence and evaluation of evidence is another way to gain discussion marks. Remember to include at least a brief reference to evidence, otherwise the marks would be limited to 8 for this section.

Student A

> **(a)** Victim surveys involve asking people whether or not they have been a victim of crime **a**. This is compared to official statistics, which include only crimes that have been reported and recorded and there are lots of reasons why some crimes are not reported or recorded. So there is a 'dark figure' of crime that official statistics do not include.

🅔 **1/4 marks awarded a** Although the student starts with a brief outline of a valid alternative way of measuring crime, the answer then strays into a discussion of official statistics. The student should have given a little more description of victim surveys as a method and then made some direct evaluation. It would have been easy to say how victim surveys help to reveal the 'dark figure' of crime.

> **(b)** Behaviour modification is operant conditioning, so prisoners could get tokens for being good. They could then exchange the tokens for other things **a** — treats like cigarettes and watching videos **b** etc. This would then make their good behaviour more likely in the future.

🅔 **2/4 marks awarded** I mark is awarded for knowledge of behaviour modification. **a** The student says that it is based on operant conditioning and that it (use of reinforcement) makes good behaviour more likely to occur in the future. If positive reinforcement had been explicitly mentioned, the description would have been complete. **b** The application to a prison environment is only half done. There is a description of the type of privileges to be earned, but the student has not specified the desired behaviour sufficiently. 1 mark is awarded for application, giving 2 marks for this section as a whole.

> **(c)** Prison can have disastrous consequences. People often cannot get jobs once they get out and are unable to look after themselves. They might offend again to get back into prison where they feel comfortable and do not have to make decisions **a**.
> Re-offending rates are high (70%) **b** because prison is a school for crime. When a young person happens to end up in prison, he or she might be in a cell with a more hardened and experienced criminal. This means that re-offending will be high because they have learnt to be a worse criminal **c**. This means custodial sentences are not effective, but at least they keep people off the streets so the public are safe. This is called incapacitation **d**.
>
> One study showed that prison officers can be dehumanising to the prisoners and this can make them stressed and mentally ill, which means they are not being improved by prison, but the opposite **e**.
>
> So what else can be done? A system that is quite new is restorative justice. This means that offenders have to make amends to their victim or to society. This is better than prison because the person must confront the consequences of their offence and this could lead to real regret, whereas prison might make them more resentful and make them harder **f**.

ⓔ 7/12 marks awarded d The first paragraph touches on several negative effects of custodial sentencing, although these are all expressed in rather anecdotal terms. Had the student referred to institutionalisation, prisonisation or brutalisation, this might have been a more persuasive paragraph. In its present form, this paragraph is awarded some limited AO2 credit for analysis of the problems associated with custodial sentencing. In the second paragraph, AO1 credit is awarded for **b** knowledge of recidivism rates (rather vague, but 70% is approximately the figure in young males) and **d** for the point about incapacitation. **c** Some credit for analysis/evaluation is also awarded in this paragraph for the further elaboration of brutalisation. **e** The point about the effects on mental health is worthy of AO2 credit, but there is insufficient description of the study, presumably Zimbardo, for AO1 credit. **f** The final paragraph neatly compares prison with an alternative — restorative justice — and explains how the latter may offer a better solution. This is well expressed and worthy of AO2 credit. There is no real evidence here except for the brief reference to recidivism rates and Zimbardo, neither covered in any detail. Had this student accrued more than 8 marks overall, it is likely that the examiner would have reduced the mark to 8 because the answer lacks evidence (AO1 = 2, AO2 = 5).

Total for this question: 10/20 marks — approximately Grade D

Student B

> **(a)** One alternative is offender self-reporting. This is where offenders tell interviewers what other crimes they have committed. Alternatively, it might be a group of likely offenders, such as young males, and they are asked about what crimes they have committed **a**. The trouble is people might exaggerate to seem like they are tough, so the results may not be a reliable, objective measure of crimes **b**.

ⓔ 4/4 marks awarded a This answer includes a useful outline of the way of measuring crime and **b** a brief but sensible evaluative point expressed using specialist terminology. This response scores full marks.

(b) Behaviour modification is a behaviourist technique for behaviour change, which uses operant conditioning principles identified by Skinner and is based on reinforcement (reward). Use of positive reinforcement helps to encourage good behaviour in the future **a**. Prisoners could be given tokens (token economy) for working in the prison kitchen and attending classes. These could be used to buy privileges like phone calls and extra visits **b**.

ⓔ 4/4 marks awarded a Behaviour modification is clearly described using appropriate terminology. **b** The application to a prison setting is appropriate; the student describes both the desired behaviour and the type of reward to be earned in objective terms. This answer deserves full marks.

(c) Custodial sentencing is thought to have four aims. The first is reform, meaning that prison should make the offender a better person **a**. It could be argued that prison does not meet this aim as many people who go into prison re-offend within 2 years of release (Cullen and Minchin, 2000) **b**. This figure is especially high for young males, 76% of whom re-offend. This suggests that the second aim of deterrence is not being met either **d**. Deterrence means to put people off offending **a**. Certainly the many who re-offend are not deterred by the prospect of another prison sentence.

The third aim of prison is incapacitation – the offender is prevented from carrying out further offences while serving a sentence **a**. This aim is met in as much as the public is safe for the duration of the offender's sentence, but as most sentences are short and many prisoners are released early, even this aim is not met **e**.

The final aim of sentencing is retribution. This means society getting its own back and making the offender pay **a**. Davis and Raymond suggested that retribution is the main purpose served by prison sentences. However, perhaps there are better ways to make offenders pay back to society. They could make good what they did by apologising to the victim and even paying them back in real terms or financially **c**. This brings victim and offender face to face and may result in true remorse as the offender empathises with their victim and sees the consequences of his or her crime, something that prison does not do. Systems of restorative justice bring offenders and victims together in this way for psychological healing. Sherman and Strang (2007) compared restorative justice and conventional programmes and found that it reduced recidivism and benefited victims who had less desire for revenge and lower stress levels **b f**.

The overall effectiveness of custodial sentencing probably depends on whether the offender gets any treatment while in prison. If prisoners attend classes like anger management that can help them to understand their behaviour and maybe change it in the future, then prison would be worthwhile. Sadly, prisons are overcrowded (population is currently over 80,000) and resources are stretched, so many prisoners do not get any treatment or education inside **g**.

In this case, it might be better to keep them out of prison but under some form of supervision, like probation. A recent idea is ankle tagging. This makes sure offenders keep a night curfew, incapacitating them from further offending in a similar way to prison **c**. Cassidy (2005) found tagging was effective in preventing breach of conditions imposed by the court, decreasing breaches by 7% **b**. However, unlike when in prison, offenders can maintain family relationships, helping them to keep out of trouble in the future and preventing them from being hardened by prison **h**. In conclusion, prison does not seem to meet the aims and perhaps there are other alternatives that are just as effective.

ⓔ **12/12 marks awarded** This student shows ample knowledge for the full 4 marks. **a** There is a clear outline of the four aims of custodial sentencing and **b** evidence in relation to recidivism rates, restorative justice and tagging. **c** There is also some description of alternatives. The discussion is wide-ranging and appears throughout the answer. **d** In the first paragraph, discussion marks are awarded for explanations of how prison neither reforms nor deters. **e** In the second paragraph, the student explores the issue of incapacitation and gains further credit for discussion. **f** The third paragraph is a highly effective comparison of prison and restorative justice, worthy of considerable AO2 credit. **g** In the fourth paragraph, the student makes the point that prison could be positive but rarely is because so many prisoners get no treatment or education. This discussion of possibilities for improvements while in prison gains further credit for analysis. Note how this leads on to the next paragraph, where the student talks about another alternative and again compares it effectively with prison. **h** This discussion of tagging as an alternative gains further AO2 credit; tagging is linked to incapacitation and the student explains how keeping the offender out of prison might prevent the negative effects of custodial sentencing. In all, this answer is well-structured and clearly argued (AO1 = 4, AO2 = 8).

Total for this question: 20/20 marks — Grade A

ⓔ **Consistent performance at this level would merit an A* grade providing other A* requirements are met.**

Knowledge check answers

1 Imitation, interactional synchrony, physical contact, modified language, sensitive responsiveness.

2 A good internal working model is important because it acts as a template for all future relationships.

3 Privation: never having had an attachment. Deprivation: having had an attachment and lost it. Privation is more damaging than deprivation.

4 Schaffer found multiple attachments, contradicting Bowlby's monotropy theory.

5 They could have used content analysis, categorising stories for themes etc. Two researchers could have coded the stories independently to check for reliability.

6 A natural observation. Strength: high ecological validity. Limitation: lack of control.

7 Piaget: the toy was deliberately taken so perhaps the child thought it was forbidden. Bower and Wishart: the disappearance was more subtle so the child would not have thought that the toy was forbidden.

8 Conservation, class inclusion and egocentrism.

9 Materials/opportunities should be provided so the child can learn through self-discovery. Each child should progress at his or her own rate. New concepts should be introduced only when the child is ready.

10 The child learns through interaction with and support from a more knowledgeable other (child as apprentice). The child learns to appreciate the world from the point of view of others (child internalises the others' world view).

11 The studies showed that young children understand objects continue to exist when out of sight (contrary to Piaget's theory of lack of object permanence).

12 Siegler argued that people develop increasingly sophisticated problem-solving strategies. Sometimes we use more sophisticated strategies; at other times we revert to less sophisticated strategies, so the strategies overlap.

13 Moral realism: judging by consequence, relying on the moral view of others. Moral relativism: judging by intention, establishing one's own moral view.

14 Moral comparisons: the listener chooses who is the most naughty and explains why. Moral dilemmas: the listener decides whether a course of action is morally right or not, and says why.

15 Moral decisions reflect social conventions i.e. what most people find acceptable.

16 Gilligan's research focused on real-life dilemmas; other research involved hypothetical dilemmas.

17 Damon focused on sharing.

18 Kohlberg and Freud assumed female reasoning was less sophisticated than male reasoning. Kohlberg: females focused on emotion and were stuck at stage three. Freud: females identified less strongly with same-sex parent than males so had a weaker superego.

19 Structural encoding; FRU activation; PIN activation; name generation.

20 Absolute judgement: witness identifies suspect without comparing to other possible suspects. Relative judgement: witness chooses person from line-up, comparing with others.

21 Leading questions; post-event discussion.

22 Reinstating context; reporting every detail; recalling events in different order; recalling from different perspective.

23 Perhaps they were embarrassed or consciously chose not to discuss something upsetting.

24 Motivated forgetting: unpleasant events cannot be accessed because they are in the unconscious.

25 Disorganised: bizarre behaviour; Catatonic: stupor; Paranoid: delusions; Residual: social withdrawal; Undifferentiated type: no key symptom.

26 (i) 100%   (ii) 50%

27 Schizophrenogenic mother; double-bind communication; high expressed emotion.

28 Strengths: greater autonomy, more 'normal' environment. Limitations: poor supervision of medication and exposure to negative attitudes in the community.

29 MAOIs, tricyclics, SSRIs, plus lithium carbonate for bipolar disorder.

30 (i) Therapist discusses reasons why client feels worthless; (ii) therapist helps client formulate a hypothesis to test; (iii) therapist encourages client to collect evidence in support of the hypothesis.

31 Adrenal medulla: releases adrenaline and noradrenaline, increasing heart rate and blood flow. Hypothalamus: produces CRF, stimulating pituitary gland to secrete ACTH, which stimulates the adrenal cortex to produce corticosteroids.

32 Physiological (e.g. heart rate); behavioural (e.g. stuttering); self-report (e.g. questionnaire).

33 (i) Committed to family, community etc; (ii) sees events as a challenge; (iii) feels in control of life.

34 (i) Problem-focused: go to the job centre; (ii) emotion-focused: go out to drown sorrows.

35 Defence mechanisms help avoid stress in the short term, but avoidance means the situation may become worse (e.g. better to deal with debt sooner than to go into denial and let it accumulate).

36 Biofeedback; systematic desensitisation.

37 Tolerance: the body adapts to the substance so more is needed for same physical/psychological effects. Withdrawal: unpleasant physical/psychological side effects when use of the drug is suddenly stopped.

38 Stimulants: ecstasy and cocaine. Depressants: alcohol and heroin.

39 Aversion therapy, based on classical conditioning. Contingency training, based on operant conditioning.

40 High fear messages: people tend to think it won't happen to them. Low fear messages: insufficiently arousing to be off-putting. Medium fear messages: arousing but not off-putting. This relationship between level of fear and effectiveness is an inverted U effect.

41 Informing about negative effects; discussion about peer pressure; skill development to resist peer criticism; public commitment.

42 Pre-contemplation; contemplation; preparation; action; maintenance; termination.

Knowledge check answers

43 Any valid example e.g. homosexuality used to be a crime in the UK but is no longer a crime.

44 The 'organised' offender shows planning, targeting a stranger and leaving little evidence. Typical characteristics include social competence, skilled job, living with a partner.

45 Atavistic form: Lombroso's view of offenders as a separate, primitive species with physical anomalies. Mesomorph: Sheldon's criminal type, muscular and aggressive.

46 Differential association theory: offending is learnt and depends on the values and norms of people with whom we associate e.g. peer group.

47 Primary reinforcers are in themselves rewarding (e.g. food). Secondary reinforcers (e.g. tokens) acquire their reinforcing properties only because they can be exchanged for primary reinforcers.

48 Cognitive preparation; skill acquisition; application practice.

Index